MONEY IN YOUR ATTIC:

How to Turn Your Furniture, Antiques, Silver and Collectibles into Cash

Helaine Fendelman
and Jeri Schwartz

in collaboration with
Beverly Jacobson

A MONARCH BOOK
Published by Prentice Hall Press
New York, NY 10023

A Monarch Book
Published by Prentice Hall Press
A Division of Simon & Schuster, Inc.
Gulf+Western Building
One Gulf+Western Plaza
New York, New York 10023

PRENTICE HALL PRESS is a trademark of
Simon & Schuster, Inc.

Designed by Publishing Synthesis, Ltd./Kenneth R. Ekkens

Manufactured in the United States of America
3 4 5 6 7 8 9 10

Library of Congress Catalog Card Number: 85-61361
ISBN: 0-671-55606-1

Contents

Introduction

How Fendelman and Schwartz Changed My Life

I was minding my own business, writing a magazine article about parasites, when the phone rang and my friend said she was sending me two ladies who were in need of a writer. Two days later, Helaine Fendelman and Jeri Schwartz arrived with a bright red paper place mat covered with scribbles that they wanted me to turn into a book.

They have rotten handwriting and, with both of them talking at once, all I could gather was that since they had joined forces in 1981 to create Fendelman and Schwartz, an arts, antiques, household appraisal and sales firm, they've had a series of hysterical, horrendous, funny, moving, sad, exhausting, instructive, and thought-provoking experiences.

The fact that they were immensely enjoying their work did not seem to me to be sufficient reason for a book. I told them that it was a terrible idea. Schwartz and Fendelman exchanged looks. Jeri gazed at the silver picture frame on the corner table and said, "Where did you get that?"

"It belonged to my mother."

"Any idea what it's worth now?"

"No. Not much, maybe $25."

"Try $150."

"Oh, come on. I distinctly remember my mother saying she bought it on sale for a song."

"Well, the song is now a symphony," smiled Schwartz. "Let's see what else you have."

I went into the kitchen for the sterling silver water pitcher I had just polished in preparation for Christmas dinner. Jeri turned it over, whipped out her jeweler's eye piece, nodded, and said, "$350, if you have that dent removed."

I made a deal right then and there for an appraisal. The first opening they had was not for a month, but when I laid down the law— no appraisal, no book—they worked me into their busy schedule sooner.

My sterling had been put away for more than a decade, ever since I exchanged the life of a suburban hostess for that of a professional writer. (Professional writers have neither the time to polish silver, nor the money to entertain and use it.) The stuff was filthy. I could have just cleaned the hallmarks, but hallmarks are funny items, they are not always in the same place, and by the time you polish a few spots looking for them, the silver appears to have caught chicken pox. Besides, my middle class background intervened. How could I let anyone see my silver in that condition? So, on and off all week, whenever I had a spare minute, I polished. Candlesticks, trays, flatware, the coffee service, pitchers, cocktail shakers, compote dishes, candy dishes, salt and pepper shakers, bread trays, vegetable servers—you name it, I had it, thanks to a long line of acquisitive ancestors. The dirt collected under my nails; the skin on my hands began to look like Scarlett O'Hara's when she was grubbing carrots at Tara right after the Civil War. But there was a fun element as well. Jeri had left me a book on silver, and every time I unearthed a hallmark, I tried to figure out if the piece were English or American, old, recent, or antique (please God).

By the time they returned one cloudy December morning, the silver had been transformed. Unfortunately, so had I! I looked like a female version of the elephant man: my face was double its normal size and I could barely see out of either eye.

Fendelman and Schwartz are nothing if not polite. Making believe I was the same person they had met two weeks before, they followed me down the basement stairs to my glorious silver show.

"It's been put away for so long, I'd forgotten how pretty it is," I said, trying to smile with this strange, uncomfortable face.

"Who polished all this?" Jeri asked.

"I did."

"Silver polish poisoning," they chimed.

"So that's it," I cried, thankful to have a disease with a name. "Is there a cure?"

"You better get some cortisone ointment right away," said Helaine.

They conducted the appraisal with care, starting with the silver. Twenty thousand dollars later Jeri said, "You better call your insurance agent right away. Christmas is a big robbery season."

When they had finished crawling under antique tables, inspecting the backs of early American chests and photographing certain lithographs, they departed, promising a written appraisal in one week. It was midafternoon and already darkening. I rushed to the phone; I didn't know who to call first, the insurance agent or the druggist. No one will ever know whether health or materialism triumphed. But $20,000 could be converted into a word processor, a trip to Europe, a paint job for the living room and sun porch, and even the repair of my front walk, which has slowly been sinking toward oblivion for years. Instantly, I had become an appraisal advocate.

What a terrific idea for a book, I thought. And, after I had carefully gone over the notes on the red paper place mat, and interviewed Fendelman and Schwartz with some degree of seriousness, I realized how much valuable information our book would contain, all of which you can discover simply by turning over this page.

Beverly Jacobson

Chapter 1

Collectibles: Don't Throw Anything Away

Everyone has his own convenient mechanism for dividing up the human race; for example, there are those who can give directions and those who cannot, those who turn up the thermostat and those who like to freeze, those obsessed with disaster versus the pathologically cheerful.

The true dividing line is simpler. People are either Packrats or Divestors. This chapter is dedicated to the Packrats of the world, without whom the word collectible would never have been coined.

Why Be a Packrat?

In a nomadic society, Divestors may be the chosen people, but, for America in the eighties, if you are not a Packrat, you are going to miss out on the Great Collectible Craze. Of course, you can become one.

Example: Barbie dolls. Little girls in the late fifties and early sixties, who were perfectly reasonable in all other matters, would go bananas right in the middle of the toy store if Mom refused to buy Barbie a new ball gown of pink net. It did not matter that Barbie already had a long, black dinner dress and two other ball gowns.

And it wasn't just Barbie—there was her boyfriend, Ken; all of her other pals (Midge, Francie, Casey, Julia, and Skipper); Ken's jeep, convertible, and battle fatigues; and suitable carrying cases for the lot of them, so that sleep-over dates could be more fun.

Barbie dolls undoubtedly brought intense pleasure to millions of materialistic American children, but their real purpose was to bankrupt the parents of these baby boomers. No wonder those parents, thrown precipitously into the antimaterialism of the Vietnam era, when their offspring wore the same pair of blue jeans for all four years of high school, packed Barbie and Ken off to the town dump with a sigh of relief.

They should not have done it.

Let's say you were fortunate enough to give birth to quintuplet girls in 1954. Let's say all of them clamored for Barbie dolls as soon as they were able to speak in sentences. Let's say you were an old softie and bought them original Barbie dolls, the ones that first appeared in 1958 and 1959. Let's say you had a big attic and are a Packrat.

Those Barbies, with blonde or brunette ponytails and curly bangs, wearing gold hoop earrings and black and white striped bathing suits, in mint condition, with their stands and original boxes, can cost a collector determined to have one—hang on now—$1,000 each.

It's Not Too Late

Please, don't feel terrible if you've misplaced your Barbie dolls. You have a lot of company. In 1967, Barbie's manufacturer, the Mattel Company, announced a trade-in program so that they could offer a new, bendable Barbie, and 1,250,000 stiff Barbies came dancing into the factory.

Fortunately, it is not too late. Barbie is still a super star in the world of toys, so big that, at the 1985 Toy Fair in New York City, Mattel gave a black-tie dinner at the Waldorf-Astoria to celebrate her birthday. (Vogue's Ginny and Ideal's Judy Garland and Deanna Durbin dolls were not invited, even though they knew Barbie when.) Of course, Oscar de la Renta, who now designs Barbie's wardrobe, was there, as were actresses Suzette Charles, Cathy Lee Crosby, Rebecca Holden and Genie Francis, who modeled full-size versions of Barbie's clothes, including evening gowns like the pink net of the fifties.

There are still plenty of little girls clamoring for 1985 Barbies, for whom they can now buy a briefcase, complete with an American Express Gold Card, that she can take to work, and a Nautilis exercise machine to help her stay in shape. BUY! These sophisticated Barbies are sure to become collectibles.

Stop!

We tell you all this so that you will stop dead in your tracks and take the title of this chapter seriously. It should be in the same category as the information Moses picked up on Mount Sinai. Don't throw anything away!

Never mind if you like neatness; you can make neat piles of everything you think will never increase in value. You can build shelves and closets in your basement and attic, and stack things. You can wait. It is the ability to wait that is the prime weapon of the serious collector. Because you can be pretty sure that the people who do not read this book will continue to contribute to the steady stream of garbage that threatens to bury our society. The whole point is—let the illiterate throw away. Sooner or later, what you save will become a collectible.

What Are "Collectibles"?

According to Harry L. Rinker, editor-in-chief of the 1984 edition of Warman's *Americana & Collectibles,* an object must meet four standards to be considered a collectible. It must have been mass produced, in the twentieth century, at low cost (a few cents to $100), and either made in America or widely collected here. Having said that, Rinker backtracks at once to admit that items meeting only two of the criteria are often considered collectible, and adds a fifth component, which he calls attitude.

For example, he collects objects relating to the American canal movement. His dark blue English Staffordshire pieces, made in the 1820s to commemorate the opening of the Erie Canal, are considered blue-chip antiques by owners of Staffordshire. But Rinker prefers to think of them as collectibles. If Rinker can make his own rules, so can you.

And so can we. Collectibles is an overworked word. In the February 1985 issue of *The Robb Report,* the magazine for connoisseurs, it is used to cover everything from antiques to gems, jewelry, silver, stamps, furniture, fine art, and ceramics. We define it somewhat more broadly than Rinker. If you've got, or intend to get, two of anything, you've got collectibles.

Collectible Art

Art historian Steven Naifeh, author of *The Bargain Hunter's Guide to Art Collecting*, thinks the collectibles market has gotten out of hand. Pointing out that some dolls made by the Bru firm in France now sell for more than $20,000 each, Naifeh says prospective collectors should consider another requirement when deciding what to collect—aesthetics. His point is that there are art bargains out there costing between $10 and $10,000 which are intrinsically lovely. Why settle, asks Naifeh, for Hollywoodiana (stuffed gorillas, Donald Duck banks, Judy Garland's red slippers from the Wizard of Oz) when you can collect "objects of enduring beauty," such as sculptures, carpets, paintings, prints, photographs, posters, and porcelain for the same money?

A Collector's Homework

However, while Naifeh clearly thinks collecting art is "better than beer cans and baseball cards," his advice on how to go about it might give one pause.

For example, here are some things you have to do to become a successful art collector. First, pick a price range you can afford; authorities agree that no more than ten percent of your assets should go into collecting art. (If you have no assets, skip to page 9.) Then pick a field within that price range and learn as much as you can about it. How? Take a couple of art history courses, visit dealers and museums, find experts whose brains you can pick, attend auctions, not to buy (that's for when you are an expert yourself), but to learn what art objects in your field are worth and how the auction process works.

Once you have decided what to collect, haunt the galleries and dealers who know about your area. Naifeh says dealers are willing, available, and anxious to be helpful because they want to develop customers. While somewhat more difficult, he also advises locating the scholars and museum curators who are the recognized experts in your field and following them around, Pied Piper style, until they break down and talk to you. Read everything in sight. Train your eye by visiting museums and galleries.

Learn how to price objects. All you need to do this is knowledge about the following twenty subjects: quality, style, artist, typicality, rarity, historical importance, certainty of attribution, authenticity, provenance, condition, medium, subject, size, signature and date, seller, time of sale, site of sale, laws governing sale, publicity, and chance.

It also helps to know how to use an ultraviolet (UV) light and to keep a magnifying glass (with a magnification factor of ten to fifteen) and a battery-operated flashlight in your back pocket or purse at all times.

Now, if you can quit your job, send your children to boarding school, give up television, movies and the theater, avoid your friends, ignore your in-laws, stop cleaning your house and cutting your lawn, and never waste time shoveling snow no matter how deep it gets, you might have the time to become expert enough in your field to make the right aesthetic and investment choices. You might, but you might also end up needing psychiatric care. Therefore, no one will blame you if you decide it is easier to collect Minnie Mouse watches, hatpins, roulette equipment, judges' gavels, or cheating devices.

Or Posters

Jack Rennert, a poster collector, dealer and owner of Poster Auctions International in New York City, disagrees with all this nonsense about acquiring expertise. Collect contemporary advertising posters, he advises, and you cannot go wrong. He means those posters that you see on subways and buses, on billboards, and on the street. "If they are graphically beautiful," he insists, "if they grab you, that's all that matters."

Pointing out that no one, eighty years ago, guessed that the commercial posters of that era would one day be considered "art," or that they would command today's hefty prices, Rennert advises would-be collectors to imitate their clever predecessors.

"The nice thing about poster collecting is that you don't have to be erudite or learned," says Rennert. "It is one area where your eyes and your instincts, if you will only trust them, can provide you with immediate expertise." Rennert compares poster viewing with TV—no one has to tell you whether a program is good or bad. You know without having to run off to your local community college or library.

How to Collect Posters

The trick, according to Rennert, is not what, but how, to collect. The romantic notion that aficionados appear in the middle of the night and steal the poster of their dreams from billboards, walls, and subway trains is nonsense; poster hangers use good glue. The art of poster gathering is cerebral and athletic; the poster collector must be on call, like a doctor or a plumber. He must act the moment the poster appears.

"There is no day two in this field," warns Rennert. You have to be ready to go to the source—either to the company, museum, gallery, or theater that commissioned the poster; the public relations or advertising agency which is handling the promotion; the artist himself or his agent; the printer; or, as a last resort, the poster hanger himself, whom you can try to bribe. You have to make a terrible nuisance of yourself. In this system of superbly controlled scarcity, all the collector can do is put on his roller skates and fly.

It was not always this way. In the Paris of 1900, there were poster dealers who would pay printers to produce additional copies, which they would then sell to collectors.

"That's the reason we have so many turn-of-the-century French posters," observes Rennert.

Compare that to the situation of the 1948 poster Ben Shahn created for Henry Wallace's independent presidential campaign. It showed Truman playing the piano and Dewey lying across the top of it singing. The message, for those of you who are too young to remember ancient American political history, was that there is no difference between the major candidates; therefore, vote for Wallace.

Says Rennert, "While no one knows how many of these posters were printed, it was not a limited edition; there could have been hundreds or even thousands. That poster is worth $3,000 today but I can't find any of them. I have a long list of customers who want them but in twenty-two years of collecting, I have seen only one, which was auctioned at Phillips five years ago. It is considered rarer than many hundred-year-old posters."

Rennert advises against collecting art posters because they generally do not appreciate in value the way advertising posters do. There are exceptions, of course: Picasso did a few that are expensive today; the Chagall posters commemorating the opening of Lincoln Center in the sixties, which sold then for $50, have brought as much as $800 to $1,000 at auction; the Ben Shahn 1963 Philharmonic Hall poster, originally $5, costs $500 now. But you must have an unbeatable combination—a famous artist, a beautiful poster, and an important event—to strike it rich, and that rarely happens.

Knowledge is Usually Power

Not everyone agrees with Rennert; most collectors and dealers advise learning as much as you can about whatever it is you decide to collect. Even Rennert admits that you will have more fun with your posters if you know something about the artist, the product or event being advertised, and the social milieu for which the poster was created. "I have no objection to people reading any of the twenty books I've written on poster art," he laughs.

Other authorities insist that knowledge is the collector's chief protection. If you don't know your field, they warn, you will be taken over the financial coals by every charlatan who haunts flea markets, every unscrupulous dealer, and every self-appointed appraiser masquerading as a true expert.

Knowledge and Value

Knowledge will also help you to locate some really good buys in the art world. *International Herald Tribune* columnist Souren Melikian, a long time observer of the auction scene, sees a split-level art market developing, divided sharply between works of famous artists which, whether aesthetically viable or not, command huge prices, and "objects of exceptional quality that are going for quite reasonable prices."

Now, you must remember that "reasonable" is relative in the fine arts field. Melikian is comparing a run-of-the-mill Monet landscape, which went for $2,400,000 at auction, with a painting by Camille Pissarro, called *A Haystack at Eragny,* which sold for a mere $154,000. Although the latter was finer quality, she writes, it did not "make a shred of difference." The problem according to Melikian is that when someone says Monet, collectors crumble, whisking out their gold fountain pens and embossed checkbooks.

Melikian's argument does have a point even for those of us who will never spend this kind of money. If knowledge is power, then the best way to achieve it is through your own interest. The bottom line in collecting is finding what turns you on, makes you want to learn more, or awakens the Compulsion to Own Syndrome, which might temporarily be lying dormant within your acquisitive soul.

Actor James Coco, who collects everything from show business memorabilia to Etruscan pottery, Victorian silver, and paintings by the New York theatrical and cabaret artist Reginald Marsh, summed up this feeling in an interview published last year in *Collectibles Illustrated.*

Said Coco, "What I am happiest about in my life is that I grew up to be what I wanted. I always was in awe of show business, and the nostalgia I have about it is part of my roots. And I am the same way about collecting as I am about acting. When there's something that I really want, I won't be talked out of it. I'll spot something, and just have to have it."

Why Everyone Is Collecting

Why has collecting hit manic proportions in contemporary America? Several factors have converged: forty years of planned obsolescence; a well-educated society with leisure time; excess disposable income; instantly available information about practically everything; finely honed advertising skills; and the desire of ordinary people to make some sort of individual statement about who they are and what they like. This is why tag sales, auctions, antique shows, flea markets, and thrift shops have become a major mid-twentieth-century phenomenon.

What Do People Collect?

Everything—literally everything. From the well known categories of stamps, coins, and art, to teddy bears, reamers (of citrus fruit), cowboy hero mementos, dinosaurabilia, cookie cutters, presidential items, Christmas tree decorations, Wacky Packies, and figural tape measures to mention only an infinitesimal sampling.

Warman's *Americana & Collectibles* runs over five hundred pages, and contains, throughout its fact-filled pages, information on other reference works, as well as the names of specialized book dealers who carry these volumes.

The Where to Sell Anything and Everything Book gives readers the names and addresses of collectors who will buy everything from string holders to shot glasses. If an object possesses a name, it probably has a collector.

Why Do People Collect?

Because it's fun. Collecting enriches life, broadens one's interests, and fills leisure time. It is an outlet for excess disposable income (or a quick route to bankruptcy if you're not careful), and can occasionally be an investment that really pays off.

Collecting also provides the excitement of the chase to a sedentary, urban society whose only other form of adrenalin-producing activity is to run after, or away from, contemporary muggers. A brilliant surgeon and art collector we know once confessed that the most exciting thing in his life, besides the operating room, was an art auction at Sotheby Parke Bernet.

Collectors Go Anywhere

A housewife in her sixties says that the best part of the collection of presidential memorabilia she and her doctor-husband put together over a seventeen-year period was the chase. "We would go anywhere."

"It took us seven years to get this rare Lincoln-Hamlin button from the 1860 campaign," she says, explaining that its value is great because Lincoln and his vice-president appear side by side. "A postmistress in New Hampshire had put it in the corner of a display of campaign buttons, where you couldn't even see it, but we must have made two dozen trips there before convincing her to sell."

It was the same with the brass George Washington inaugural button owned by an auto mechanic in Lebanon, New Hampshire*, who had bought it for $10 in 1939. The bright, round disc features Washington's image, surrounded by the inscription, "Long Live the President," with the initials of the thirteen original colonies carved around the periphery. In 1789, it was fashionable to wear these inaugurals either as lapel buttons or lockets; in fact, there were five or six versions made. It took six trips to Lebanon, and a free physical from the doctor, before the mechanic agreed to part with it.

But her favorite acquisition story concerns the statue of Rutherford B. Hayes, which stands in the living room of their ranch-style house. The four-foot-high statuette of President Hayes was created for his 1876 centennial presidential campaign. Hayes is dressed in a smashing red jacket and sports a neat, graying Van Dyke beard. A dealer in Framingham, Massachusetts, who had heard about this couple's penchant for things presidential through his contacts in APIC (the American Political Items Collectors), phoned one day with the offer of Hayes. They sent him a check at once and arranged for the exchange to take place at the doctor's office. When the dealer arrived, no one was there, so he put Rutherford in a body bag and left him hanging from the front door knocker.

Nostalgia and Collecting

When Philip V. Snyder was a boy, what he remembers is his grandfather's Christmas tree ornaments. They represented much of the spectrum that was available in the good old days such as lovely light

---

* All locations have been changed or invented to protect the clients' privacy.

glass balls; tiny glass figures of children's favorite storybook characters, miniature animals, houses, and churches; and figures, miniature coaches, carriages and steam engines, even a four-inch Wright Brothers airplane, that were made from pressed gold and silver Dresden cardboard.*

No wonder, then, that he grew up not only to inherit his grandfather's collection, but also to expand it to several thousand pieces, and to write two volumes about his hobby, *The Christmas Tree Book* and *December 25*.

"Celebrating Christmas with trees, ornaments, and Santa Claus did not occur in this country until the 1850s," says Synder. It was brought here by German and Pennsylvania Dutch immigrants at the time of the Civil War. Before then, American Christmases were puritanical affairs because "the Founders were dissenters, who did not want to have anything to do with Christmas."

But, by 1890, these new citizens had helped to create a cultural revolution that culminated in the Victorian Christmas. Christmas trees were in vogue and entire glass villages shimmered on them. It is hard for contemporary Americans, conditioned by sterile, mass-produced, multi-colored globes, which shatter if the cat so much as walks into the room, to imagine what an old-fashioned Christmas tree looked like. But New Yorkers and tourists who visit the city during the Christmas season, can see one at the Gotham Book Mart, 41 West 47th Street, because owner Andreas Brown is another ornament collector with fond memories of childhood Christmases.

Nostalgia seems to drive all ornament collectors. Snyder tells a story about a big league colleague, with sixteen thousand items in his collection, who admitted that he was still searching for three decorations that had adorned his childhood tree. The most elusive, the one he had been dreaming of, was a bear with a broom. Snyder smiled when he heard this, went to his bear drawer, pulled that very ornament out and gave it to the frustrated collector. The man could hardly believe his good fortune, or the fact that, within a year, Snyder had located five more bears with brooms.

*Dresden cardboard refers to silver or gilt cardboard ornaments, manufactured using the same technology that was employed to make Victorian candy boxes; that is, raised three dimensional cardboard which is stamped when wet. These ornaments are also sometimes painted.

Snyder says incredible ornaments have surfaced in the last five years because of an increased interest in Christmas and higher prices. "But," he maintains, "the nice thing about collecting Christmas ornaments is that beautiful, pre-1950 examples can still be found for between $10 and $20."

Teddy Bear Tales

Teddy bear collectors also have nostalgic souls. As a child, Cindy Ross dressed stuffed animals rather than dolls; today her passion is teddy bears. She started collecting miniature bears and has several hundred of these. Four years ago, she fell in love with two full-size bears because one had a "goofy" face and the other was "so soft and cuddly."

Today she has about sixty large bears, which she displays in a 1913 Sears Roebuck child's wicker stroller, on the fireplace mantel, the coffee table, and in numerous hanging shelves around her apartment. Her husband, who approves of her hobby, says his only fear is that one night he'll wake up and find they're all alive.

Bear authorities Pia and Alan Bialosky, authors of *The Teddy Bear Catalog* and, with Robert Pine, *Making Your Own Teddy Bears,* live in a place called Novelty, Ohio, whether by design or chance they won't say. There, besides researching bears, pricing bears, and loving bears, Pia also makes them. Her favorite story concerns the day she needed a prop for a bear she was creating and cut out a piece of the lining of Alan's old raincoat.

"I was so proud of myself for making a fully jointed teddy bear in four and a half hours, until Alan came home and pointed out that I had grabbed the wrong raincoat. Now he wears his new Burberry with this teddy bear shape cut out of the lining."

If you are lucky enough to have anything left from your childhood, think twice before selling it, because it's a piece of yourself; the minute it's gone, you'll probably want it back.

Coins and Carnivals

Nostalgia for his youthful visits to the Rock Springs Amusement Park in Chester, West Virginia, may have been what started Dr. James

Smith's interest in arcade machines, but the additional benefits have been considerable. One is an embellished sense of history; the second, a family involvement that has been a source of delight.

Twenty years of poking around the entire United States by Dr. Smith and various members of his clan have resulted in one of the largest collections of coin-operated machines in the world. It has also produced an impromptu sabbatical for James Smith III (Jim), the eldest of the five Smith children, who has postponed his graduate studies to put the collection, previously stored in the family home and several trailers, in order.

Now filling an eighteenth-century barn in Greenwich, Connecticut, this museum-quality collection contains over five hundred examples of American carnival, fair, and circus history. There are four Wurlitzer band organs; six of the fourteen lung testers known to exist in the world; a double Violano-Virtuoso, where two violins and a piano play twenty thousand popular and classical selections mechanically; the famous Cardiff Giant, a papier-maché statue that P.T. Barnum tried to pawn off on the American public as the petrified corpse of a prehistoric man; and the ringmaster, trapeze artist, and elephant head from the now defunct Danbury State Fair in Connecticut.

Jim Smith remembers "growing up with these machines," but he also recalls nearly ending up in a New Mexico jail when he and his friends were stopped by police, who wanted to know why the devil they had half a dozen slot machines in the back of their truck. It took four hours and several long distance calls before Smith was able to prove that he was really delivering them to a bonafide museum.

Slot Machines Are Ancient History

Contrary to what you might think, slot machines were not invented in the saloons and carnivals of the American West. They actually first appeared in ancient Egypt where, according to researchers Fran and Ken Rubin, penitents could receive some holy water with the deposit of a few drachmas. The Romans also used them. Coin operated machines then went underground, resurfacing in eighteenth-century England, where they offered tobacco and snuff for the proper quantity of pence.

Their American debut occurred in 1839; the first arcade machines dispensed tobacco but they quickly graduated to gambling. Prohibition put a big dent in their use because it closed the bars where the slot machines flourished. Television more or less finished them off, until the various space movies caused a revival that has been bankrupting American kids ever since.

Much of this history can be found in the large reference area in the Smith's barn, where restoration and research are still underway. Unfortunately, there is no plan to open the collection to the public because there is too much maintenance involved.

Uncommon Collectibles

You think no one collects Chinese firecracker labels and catalogs? You are wrong. A man in North Dakota, who is big in the Pyrotechnic Guild International, does.

What about infant or invalid feeders? John Margulies, of Floral Park, New York, has more than seven hundred of them, and publishes a newsletter called *The Feeder's Digest*. He is one of an estimated one hundred collectors in the United States and Canada.

Margulies says that no one knows if these quaint vessels were first used as infant or invalid feeders, but they have been found in graves, particularly those of children, from Etruscan, Roman, and Egyptian times. An article in the July-August issue of *Colonial Homes* refers to them as baby feeders, which were filled with pap and panada, two gruel-like concoctions, and hand held for infants starting in the sixteenth century. They are also known as papboats.

Before the invention of the baby bottle, these little feeders were a standard part of every set of dishes; therefore, they can be found in ceramic, glass, metal, pottery, china, ironstone, porcelain, tin enamel, plastic, pewter, and all grades of silver.

Invalid feeders are still used for nourishing patients in parts of Europe. In fact, one of the joys of traveling abroad for these collectors is locating new and antique feeders in unlikely places. In the last few years, Margulies has found, or been given by traveling friends, feeders from Russia, Mexico, Bavaria, and Portugal. And episode six of Masterpiece Theater's *The Jewel and The Crown* gave these collectors an enormous boost as they recognized the object which Sarah Layton handed to Ronald Merrick, when he asked for a drink in his Capetown hospital room, as a genuine invalid feeder.

Some feeders resemble miniature gravy boats without their trays, but they actually come in all shapes. There is an elongated version, the Aladdin's lamp, with the spout on one side and the handle on the other; the round bowl or cup shape, with a handle to the right of the spout and a cover across half of the top; the vertical shape, which is more like a drinking glass, taller than wide; and the teapot shape, which is no longer manufactured. Some come in the form of animals—ducks, birds, or the head of an elephant, with the trunk as a spout.

Not Even the Streets Are Safe

Cobblestones have been collectibles for at least two decades, but a new twist was introduced this year when authorities in New York City discovered that "someone has been tearing up some of the city's oldest streets, paving stone by paving stone, and carting them away. Neither the police nor city officials know who is responsible." Affected areas included streets paved with Belgian granite stones from the 1800s, as well as those done with flat paving stones manufactured in 1940.

Any collector could have told officials that the culprits had to be thieves. Collectors would have known the difference between the genuine Belgian cobblestones and their twentieth-century imitations, and would not have bothered to steal the latter. The police came to the same conclusion after arresting two men in the Bronx for trying "to make off with the corner of 161st Street and Jerome Avenue." (*New York Times,* January 12, 1985)

For the Birds

Margery Schwartz, an interior designer from Stamford, Connecticut, collects *whatsits*. A whatsit is "a gadget, gimcrack, or gimmick whose purpose is not immediately apparent to the uninitiated," according to *Yankee's Book of Whatsits*.

One of Margery's prize possessions is a ladies bird chaser, a wooden noisemaker from the 1800s, identical in shape to those tin and plastic objects used on New Year's Eve or at particularly rowdy children's parties. Nineteenth-century ladies in hoop skirts, when sitting in the garden, used to twirl this gadget above their heads to frighten off the birds, and thus protect themselves and their finery from what we will euphemistically refer to as the inevitable outpourings of avian creatures.

Margery knew what her bird chaser was because the dealer, from whom she bought it, told her, after considerable prodding. "That's a game whatsits people play," she says. "But if anyone can tell me what my primitive wooden Indian artifact is, I might be willing to give them a part interest in my Appalachian ear trumpet as a reward. The Indian gadget is about a foot long, with a slim, turned handle and a hollowed-out scoop shaped like a darning egg, but which comes to a point in front. It looks a little like a ladle, but about five-eights of the way up the handle there is a ratchet, which no ladle I've ever seen has or needs."

If you recognize this object, please, send us a telegram.

Too Much Information

One of our associates, collector and contemporary art expert Helene Trosky, haunts church bazaars and thrift shops looking for paintings, drawings, and lithographs. Last year she bought a painting that she believed was by a South American artist she admires named Carlos Irizarry. Cost: $2.

She spent a year researching it, writing to numerous Latin American consulates, trying to find out if hers was really an Irizarry and also some more information about the artist. No one seemed to know.

Then one day, while she was working at Alan Brown's Gallery in Hartsdale, New York, a woman came in with two wonderful paintings by Irizarry which she wanted framed. Excited, Helene asked what she knew about the painter and learned that he is from Puerto Rico.

Intrigued by the thought of discovering an unknown artist, and perhaps helping him further his career, she wrote immediately to Puerto Rico.

Haydee Venegas of the Museo De Arte De Ponce, Puerto Rico, replied with a clipping containing biographical information. Irizarry was born in Puerto Rico in 1938. He lived in New York from 1947 to 1963, where he studied commerical art and design. After returning to San Juan, he joined a gallery and participated in shows in Tokyo, Yugoslavia, Norway, Austria, Brazil, and Argentina.

As to Irizarry's present whereabouts, Venegas wrote:

> Carlos Irizarry is back in Puerto Rico. He spent two years in jail for hijacking a plane. He pledged it was a work of conceptual art or a performance. While in jail, he painted a series of wonderful portraits. They were exhibited early this year in the Institute of Puerto Rican Culture.
>
> I don't know his present whereabouts. His telephone was disconnected. As soon as I reach him, I will send him a copy of your letter.

Helene is still pondering if and how she should reply. You never know where your research will lead.

Trust Your Instincts

We hate authors who give advice in a didactic manner; even how-to books that are supposed to instruct readers should be incredibly subtle. But at this point we have got to take a stand.

It is the matter of "ins" and "outs" that has got our goat. For example, Ralph and Terry Kovel, in the February 1985 issue of *Cape Cod Antiques Monthly,* have proclaimed the following items "in" in home decor:

For the Young and Daring (YD): the fifties look (Herman Miller chairs, Noguchi or kidney bean shaped tables, Blenko glass); chairs made of cow horns or twigs; Victorian Egyptian Revival sofas with sphinx heads, obelisks and roaring lions; Navajo and old Chinese rugs. All in.

Out for the YDs: country and mission furniture (except in the Midwest or New England, where they presumably haven't heard yet); Orientals; spatter-painted floors and strip rag carpets. All out.

For pottery and procelain buffs, Ohr snake pottery is in, as are wall masks and naked lady flower holders from the thirties.

Out are Dresden figurines, Dr. Wall Worcester, and all of the late nineteenth-century German and English porcelains.

Now, this sort of thing is not so much of a problem for the Young and Daring. They are just starting out, so they can spend their time making chairs out of cow horns or twigs if they want to, or ransacking relatives' attics and antiques shops for Egyptian sofas loaded with roaring lions. They can sneer at parents who try to give them mission furniture, and throw any Dresden figurines they happen to inherit against the fireplace wall (if fireplaces are still in).

It is last year's YDs about whom we worry. There they are, spending their leisure time trying to get the spatter paint off the floors instead of being out there shopping. How will they ever have time to pick up a Navajo rug or a couple of naked lady flower holders?

We don't know what Dr. Wall did to be out, and don't intend to take sides in the matter, but we definitely predict that those naked lady flower holders are not going to last.

What's more, we think collectors should stick-to-their guns and take the annual and biennial swings of media-inspired fashion trends in stride. You've got to have taste and judgment and self-confidence to be a collector and not jump around like a frog who has lost his lily pad. So trust your instincts and, if you like Orientals, hang in there. They never show dirt and are absolutely childproof. And they'll probably be back in next year.

F & S's Quick Tips

- IT'S NEVER TOO LATE TO START COLLECTING
- SAVE EVERYTHING: NEATNESS IS NOT IMPORTANT
- COMPULSION TO OWN SYNDROME CAN BE A GOOD DISEASE
- LEARNING ABOUT WHAT YOU LIKE IS IMPORTANT
- TRUSTING YOUR COMPULSIONS IS MORE IMPORTANT
- HAVING FUN IS MOST IMPORTANT

2

The Coming Collectibles: Why You'll Never Throw Anything Away Again

We are about to join weatherpersons and sportscasters and take the plunge into predicting, a dangerous and thankless pastime. In view of our courage (we did not have to include this chapter to get the book published), we want a promise from all of you that you will not send us ripped-out pages, accompanied by angry notes, if our auguries are only eighty-three percent correct. If you won't promise, please skip to Chapter Three.

We have divided our forecasts in half. Category one covers collectibles which, although already established, will increase in value. While this is not exactly getting in through the basement window, you can be certain you are not above the first or second floor, and that the elevator is rising.

Category two is for items that will, we hope, become collectible.

Category One: Going, going, not gone, but up!

Group A:
Things that were, more or less, originally created to please small children.

1. Cabbage Patch Kids. Cabbage Patch dolls, created by Xavier Roberts and manufactured by Coleco, first appeared in June 1983. By December of that year, parents were hitting each other over the head in department store aisles trying to spend approximately $25 to bring one home for Christmas. Coleco says the shortage was not planned but reflected an overwhelming and unexpected reception by the children of America. Whatever, the scarcity of Cabbage Patch Kids became a major media event. TV reporters braved hysterical crowds to interview successful shoppers, while the failures were seen slinking out a side door and heading for the nearest bridge. By the end of 1984, Coleco had delivered twenty million Cabbage Patch Kids, one for every boy and girl between the ages of three and eight in the United States and Canada, doing more than $500 million worth of business. Retail prices for Cabbage Patchers now range between $30 and $60.

The appeal of the Kids is apparently not only their cuddly quality and wide-eyed innocence, but also their "legend." Each one is born in Babyland General Hospital (BGH), comes with a birth certificate and adoption papers, and bears a birthmark signature of Xavier Roberts on its "little bottom." Coleco guarantees its dolls— if a defective one gets out of BGH, a death certificate is issued and a replacement doll arrives instead. There is even a cemetery for Cabbage Patch Kids, not run by the company.

In 1985, Coleco introduced a number of new products: twins in a special collector's edition; world travelers, wearing the garb of their home countries, packaged in steamer trunks and equipped with airline tickets and travel brochures; playmates, five-and-one-half-inch miniature versions of the big Kids, complete with their own musical merry-go-round and buggy; and preemies, infants with pacifiers stuck in their mouths. Also available are show ponies with purebred papers, and pets called Koosas, with registration papers that can be mailed to the Koosas Kennel Association. There are accessories such as playpens, portable beds, baby carriers and swings, strollers, and a pram that holds three of the Kids at once. Finally, there is a new line of clothing, featuring designer furs and costume sleepers, and an enterprising dry-cleaning establishment in Westchester County, New York, which has a sign in its window that reads, "We Clean Cabbage Patch Clothes."

Now, it is hard to be sanguine about the collectibility of dolls produced, not by the barrel load, but by the million load. We are sure, however, that the Cabbage Patch Kids are bound for immortality and will increase in value.

We're not so certain about their "parents." We figured out that any three to eight year old who has one regular size Kid, one set of twins, one preemie, a Koosa, and a pony will be a nervous wreck by the time she/he is nine. How will the poor thing get to school with so much domestic responsibility? After that young "parent" finishes dressing her/his Cabbage Patch Kids in their fun furs and costume sleepers, taking the twins in and out of the playpen, pushing the stroller, cleaning up after the Koosa, and making sure someone exercises the pony, she/he will be in no shape to deal with long division or finger paint.

Fortunately, someone has started Camp Small Fry in Redbank, New Jersey, where exhausted "parents" can send their Cabbage Patch Kids for the summer. We don't know what it costs, but it is probably cheaper than psychoanalysis.

2. Erector sets. What can we say? Everyone knows what erector sets look like. They're collectible and increasing in value.

3. ET dolls. If you've got one, put it away. For how long? We're going to hedge on this one—Somewhere between a decade and a generation.

4. Fast food giveaways. Examples are Burger King cardboard crowns, Ronald McDonald dolls, glassware, and plastic bag-hand puppets.

5. Halloween memorabilia. Includes everything mildly orange, such as paper lanterns, streamers, party favors, original photographs of people in Halloween costumes, and books documenting Halloween customs through the ages. This collectible has escalated by several thousand percent in the last eight years, jumping from $.30 an item then, to between $30 to $200 today. Nevertheless, we think this trend will continue.

6. Measuring devices. Items such as plastic rulers, protractors, compasses, slide rulers, and weights. Thanks to the hand-held calculator and the digital scale, they are hard to find now and increasingly valuable.

Wooden rulers are particularly unique, since you have to be a grandmother to know what one looks like. One of us has a sister who walks around without a bodyguard, in spite of the presence in her knitting bag of a twelve-inch-long wooden ruler, the kind old-fashioned teachers used to employ on misbehaving knuckles and fannies before Freud taught us to avoid early trauma. When she hauls it out to measure her progress on an emerging sweater or cap, everyone under the age of thirty-five says, "What's that?" We give her plastic replacements every Christmas and beg her to lock it up in her safe-deposit box, but she stubbornly continues to use this collector's item, worth at least $5. If it had a logo on it, or was adorned with an advertiser's name such as Eisner's Paint and Hardware Store, its value would escalate to $7. It is clear you could be wealthy if you had enough rulers.

7. Product giveaways and special sales offers. Already collected and expensive are the giveaways of an earlier age. A Cracker Jack metal car, which once poured free from its sticky box, can now bring the hoarder who was clever enough to save it $45; a twenty-five-inch Planters Peanut display sign from 1930, $145; and a four-inch Little Orphan Annie bisque toothbrush holder from 1930, showing Annie and Sandy sitting side by side, not brushing anything, $95.

You don't have to pay these prices to become a collector if you are willing to become your own soothsayer. Study the coupon sections of your Sunday newspapers, the mailers that flood your home every day, and the ads in the magazines you buy. Check the special offers where the company is giving away or selling something.

8. Robots. If you have an intact robot with all of its parts in working order, put it away and wait. Look what has already happened. A 1965 twelve-inch plastic Chief Robotman is listed in Warman's at $275; Mr. Atomic Robot, circa 1955 to 1962, is $1,500.

9. Sesame Street material. Original first editions are winners.

10. Sports cards. Unopened packs only. The thing to do is to go to hobby shops and candy stores, buy them and put them away until

sometime around 2025. Don't take the kids, or even one kid, because they will have the packs open while you are still counting your change.

11. Toys. Those from the forties, fifties, and the sixties will continue to increase in value. To be really valuable, however, they should be in mint condition in their original boxes.

12. Wacky Packies. These are parodies of advertising slogans with gummed backs, which little kids used to covet, holler for, get Mom to buy, and then come home and paste all over their beds, walls, radiator covers, bureaus, desks, and closet doors. Their gummed backs used an intractable cement that preceded Crazy Glue, the kind of product that, if you got some on your hands you were web-fingered for life.

Wacky Packies advertised products like "Peter Pain Peanut Butter" and "Spills Brothers Coffee." If your youngsters lived on the third floor and you haven't been up there recently, you may find some still stuck to closet walls. You may even find a formula for removing them. (If so, write to us immediately. One of us is afflicted with leftover Wacky Packies, which she has been trying to get off radiator covers and furniture for the last fifteen years.) If you had a forgetful kid who put them away, and you locate them in their original wrappers, you have got a prize. But don't sell yet, they will only become more valuable.

An Important Message to Children Who Can Read

The sentence we most often hear from our adult friends is "Why didn't I save it?" "It" applies to everything, from their favorite bubble pipe and Dydee doll, to the first edition of *Alice in Wonderland* that somehow got sold with the family home. What we have learned from this is that parents, all parents, are busy, harassed, burdened, and vexed individuals for about twenty years, the exact time span it takes for you to grow up. They cannot be expected to stop and consider the collectibles of the future.

It is therefore up to you to take care of your dolls and toys. When you receive a new doll, for example, do not rip the box to smithereens. Save it, because a doll that is MIB (mint condition in the original box) is worth twice as much as its boxless double. Put your toys away carefully each night, preferably on shelves; never throw them at each other or into some overcrowded toy chest; do not leave them out in the rain and snow; and, when you are off to college, lock them away with your diaries in a safe house, one that won't be sold while you are taking Art History and Introduction to Space Travel.

Group B:
Items bought mostly by adolescents and college students.

1. Beatles memorabilia. What type of things? Just about everything—records, clothing, anything with a logo, posters, photographs.

2. Chuck Berry and other early rock and roll stars. Ditto.

3. Ray Charles and the Beach Boys. Ditto.

4. Elvis Presley. Ditto.

5. Mid-twentieth-century typewriters. Very shortly, these will be as quaint as a Singer sewing machine with a treadle.

6. Message tee shirts, head bands, and kerchiefs from the sixties and early seventies. These chronicle a time of great social upheaval in this country. We know a young lawyer who still won't forgive his mother for ruining his last Grateful Dead tee shirt by using it to wash the windows.

7. Pot pipes and hookahs. Those parents who made a practice of confiscating smoking supplies along with marijuana were absolutely correct, morally and legally. But if they threw them away, it was a mistake. They say something about the sixties and are now collectibles.

Group C:
Items bought by and for adults.

1. Accessories from the early twentieth century. Examples: rayon dresses of the forties, particularly those with peplums; handbags,

and hats; silk blouses; rayon and silk stockings with seams; and garter belts. Most clothing with hand-worked detail such as embroidered blouses, dresses, and handbags. Also, the almost ankle length "new look" dresses of the immediate post-World War II period.

2. Auction, museum & gallery exhibition catalogs. The best are illustrated and in mint condition. Buy these at the shows you attend and hang on to them; they will become more valuable.

3. Aviation material from World War II. These include airplane models used by blackout wardens to spot planes; jackets, helmets, and wings worn during the war; silk kerchiefs printed with the area to be bombed that were worn by pilots and navigators; and anything from civil-defense groups or bomb shelters.

4. Board games. They have been used by adults as well as children for thousands of years. Modern games go in and out of fashion quickly, and the trick is to guess which ones will lack staying power and thus become rare. They must be unused. Regarding popular games, only first editions are collectible.

5. Books on particular topics, such as regional art. Examples: books on Indiana art (for Indianians); southwestern memorabilia such as catalogs from early Indian trading posts.

6. Cinerama (3-D) glasses with cardboard frames, now worth $25 and rising.

7. Contraceptive tins. Even though no one under thirty-five recognizes such an object. If any of you saved yours, they are now worth $5 to $50.

8. Figural tape measures. These are devices which roll up into the form of animals, people, household objects, flowers, and fauna, and are made of celluloid, porcelain, wood, and ivory. They cost between $75 and $200 each.

These collectors are particularly avid. Jeri has several customers who are always searching for them. Last year she heard about two figural tape measures that were coming up for auction in London. Unable to attend herself, she sent one of her English

pickers*, who lives thirty-five miles outside of the city, to buy
Felix the Cat and the Duke of Windsor, both made of celluloid.
Total cost: $150 for the pair plus $50 in expenses. Crazy? She
doesn't think so, nor do we. We predict these will become
important and expensive collectibles and that you should all start
looking for them now.

9. Gas station giveaways. Road maps (keep taping yours with library
tape, they are getting rarer and rarer) and glasses. Also, posters and
signs from the gas wars of the fifties.

10. Hawaiian shirts from the forties are worth hundreds of dollars
today and will escalate.

11. Invalid feeders, see Chapter One.

12. Laces and linens. Tablecloths, place mats, napkins, sheets, pillow
cases, clothing, and antimacassars made of cotton and linen,
particularly if they are embroidered by hand or with lace.

13. Mementos of the sixties cultural revolution. Signs, posters, books,
buttons, newsletters, and other printed matter from communes, the
civil rights and Vietnam War protest movements, and campus
strikes, are all collectible.

14. Paper ephemera of the fifties. Things such as Valentines and
postcards.

15. Posters, see Chapter One.

16. Presidential material. Especially relating to Nixon, because he's the
only President to resign; also Kennedy, who holds a special
fascination for the American people.

17. Theatrical memorabilia. For example, costume and set designer
renderings. Those of established designers are costly and have
commanded hundreds of dollars at auction. But if you are willing
to take a chance on young designers, you can buy their renderings

* Pickers are people who uncover antiques at secret sources. They are also called
knockers, a name acquired because they used to knock on doors looking for
treasures.

for a few dollars each, either directly from them, or at Greenwich Village and Soho art galleries in New York City.

Also good are costumes of famous and emerging stars. If, while seeing *The Real Thing,* you fall in love with Jeremy Iron's bathrobe, try going to the theater and offering them $25 when the play closes. You may get it.

Movie costumes such as Judy Garland's wardrobe from the Wizard of Oz, or Marilyn Monroe's famous white dress. Hollywood studios hold costume auctions from time to time.

Props, scenery, and objects that are used by stars increase in value.

Souvenir and record albums, scripts of musicals, and theatrical posters disappear fast and become collectibles.

Early playbills are collected, but rarely command high prices.

18. Varga calendar pinup girls.

19. Wine labels by recognized artists.

Mouton Rothschild commissions artists to design labels for its Pauillac wines. Picasso did the most famous one in 1973, which is a super collectible. Labels are considered most valuable if still attached to an unopened bottle of wine. This creates a financial and epicurean problem. Can you imagine shelling out $175 for a bottle of Pauillac and not drinking it?

Labels are coaxed off bottles by soaking them in a solution of ammonia and water. They are not easy to remove and sometimes disintegrate. Figuring out how to preserve the label and enjoy the wine is part of the fun of collecting.

Some examples of Pauillac wine label art that will increase in value are:

The 1982 autographed label by John Huston, which says "to my dear Baron Phillippe on the occasion of his sixtieth birthday," retailing at $59.95.

The 1966, $175 bottle with a label by Pierre Alechinsky, the Belgian expressionist painter.

The $25, 1980 bottle with a label designed by Karl Hartung, a German abstract sculptor.

Kenwood, a West Coast vineyard, commissions a different artist each year to create labels for its Cabernet wines. In 1981, prize-winning Austrian etcher Josef Eidenberger designed the California series. This wine currently sells for about $25 a bottle. Try to find the entire series.

Group D:
Adult items for which you need room.

1. Authentic pieces from architecturally-important buildings. For example, an art deco frieze from the Bonwit Teller building in Manhattan, which, unfortunately, was demolished before the "preservation" lobby galvanized to save it. These collectors not only own large houses but also are strong.

   Such mementos will become more valuable, but if you cannot find them, you can try stocking up on authentic pieces from architecturally-unimportant buildings by visiting the new warehouse operated by the New York City Landmarks Preservation Commission. While the objects available are not pedigreed collectibles yet, we think these garden-variety newel posts, railings, balusters, window frames, and doors will become collectible because they represent an attempt at authentic restoration.

2. Magazine specials. Complete runs of certain magazines such as *Antiques,* which has been published since 1922, and *Rolling Stone.* Also certain special editions have become collectors items, like the annual "swimsuit" issue that *Sports Illustrated* has published every February since 1964, or the September 1984 issue of *Penthouse* with Vanessa Williams' photos. Early copies of *Playboy* are definitely increasing in value.

3. Regional artists. Between 1900 and 1920, many areas in this country developed regional art schools, composed of local artists, who studied with established masters, often in Europe. After returning home, they adapted what they had learned to their own interests and needs. There were six schools of American Impressionism, in California, Indiana, Boston, Philadelphia, Old Lyme, Connecticut, and New York.

   William Gerdts, noted art historian, devoted a full chapter to the Hoosier group in a recent book on American Impressionism.

These artists, T. C. Steele, Otto Stark, William Forsyth, J. O. Adams, and R. B. Gruelle, whose European educations were largely financed by Indiana businessmen, came home to paint subjects, such as farms, woods, and rivers, that were familiar and important to them.

Indiana artists are now the subject of renewed interest and research; prices of their work are starting to rise. Henry Eckert, Indianapolis art dealer, says Indiana art is still affordable, between $300 and $3000.

4. Revival furniture. After generations of chrome, formalism is returning. Just the way the Yuppies (young, urban professionals) dispatched their blue jeans and long hair, so they are eschewing the Eames chair in favor of Empire and Biedermeier furniture.

Popular during the early nineteenth century, this style of furniture was called Empire in France, correctly reflecting Napoleon's status. But Beidermeier? He wasn't a furniture mogul, designer, or cabinetmaker. He was a cartoon character in an early German humor magazine, who loved comfort so much that he came to embody the German sense of agreeability, which they call "gemutlichkeit."

It is not easy for the untrained eye to differentiate among antique Biedermeier pieces from the earliest part of the century; later examples, circa 1815 to 1835, which, though partially machine made, were beautifully hand-finished; and the totally machine-made versions produced after 1860.

The marketplace separates them, however. A lyre-shaped, drop-front antique Biedermeier desk sold at auction in New York City for $154,000 in January 1985. If that's too steep for you, try the quality department stores, where you might still find old Biedermeier pieces ranging in price from $250 to $6,500.

Biedermeier furniture will increase in value. But there are some trade-offs to be considered. For example, couples can spend $5,000 for an antique, swan-neck, narrow bedframe (the nineteenth century had a lot of goodies, but large beds were not among them), and be unique and collectible but extremely uncomfortable. Or they can settle for a Biedermeier reproduction sleigh bed for $1,200 and have room to turn over.

5. Vintage cars. Examples are Mustangs, T-birds, Corvettes, 1955–57 Chevrolets, and convertibles from the fifties and sixties with their original tops. These cars, though not particularly rare, have become collectible because of their original popularity. For example, the 1955 Chevy was the first with a V-8 engine, one that could be "souped up" for the drag racers of that era. Besides, all that many American males have to do is look at a 1957 Chevy convertible to be awash in memories of senior proms and moon-light drives.

Of the six million Chevrolets manufactured between 1955 and 1957, one million still exist, according to Dan Danchuk, owner of Danchuk Manufacturing, a firm that makes parts for these collector cars. People not only still drive them to work, they also sell those in good condition for as much as $10,000.

We think these cars will continue to go up. If you have an empty barn, are handy or have a lover who is a mechanic, and are rich, this collectible may be for you.

6. Stock market tickers. With or without glass domes.

Category Two

Okay, here is the lowdown on what will become collectible during the rest of this decade:

1. Any artistically designed promotional item which is made only once, like the 1980 Hershey eight-by-three-inch round polychrome tin with a picture of a contented mother and an angelic child on the front. If you find one, eat the kisses and save the tin.

2. Astronaut food. Currently available at the Museum of Natural History in New York and at some sporting-goods stores.

3. Calling cards. They went out of style in 1920. They are not even mentioned in Warman's. Start looking.

4. Contemporary figural telephones. For example, at the Phone Center Store in White Plains, New York, Snoopy was on sale for $114.95 in February 1985 because he is being discontinued. If you can still find him, or any other figural phone, grab it. It will definitely be a collector's item.

5. Designer clothing. Save your Bill Blass, Ralph Lauren, Gloria Vanderbilt, Anne Klein, Halston, and Calvin Klein clothes. Wear them now, but do not give them away no matter how much styles change.

   We think some of them will appreciate like the Fortuny dresses of the twenties, those sheaths you can roll into a ball without creasing them, which are now worth thousands. Gloria Vanderbilt wore one to an opening in February 1985, creating an "event" for society and fashion writers. A collector we know in Scarsdale, New York, keeps his Fortunys in a vault, and recently, Fortuny fabric sold at auction at Sotheby's for $10 an inch.

6. Designer shopping bags. Those you get free from museums, department stores, and boutiques. One of our daughters has put under lock and key a little metallic silver shopping bag she acquired after buying a ton of Ralph Lauren cosmetics. These current additions to the field of ephemera (which means anything short-lived or transitory) may not reach the status of a Kewpie postcard, which is now worth $38, but they will become collectibles. Therefore, do not use them to bring chicken soup to your ailing college freshman. Put them away in a nice, dry, childproof container and wait!

7. Disabled American Veterans (DAV) items. Things, such as key chains and address labels.

8. Early birth control pill containers.

9. Early tapes made by MTV, the national cable music channel.

10. Figural soap and candles.

11. First computers. The earliest are only for people with two barns or an eighty-four room house. If you don't believe us, run up to see the Computer Museum in Boston, where someone measured the arithmetic unit of ANFS/Q7 and logged it at thirty feet long, seven feet high, and one yard thick. We don't think there will be many collectors of these dinosaurs, but some of the first home

computers, particularly those no longer manufactured, will become collectibles.

12. Frequent flyer memorabilia. The stickers, cards, and other identifying paper ephemera from the airline companies participating in the "Great Ticket Giveaway" of the eighties. Save, particularly, the cascade of newsletters, even though you need a Ph.D. candidate to interpret instructions about the complex routes travelers may adopt to earn extra mileage.

These documents will prove that an entire generation of Americans was willing to ignore the fact that the shortest distance between two points is a straight line, in order to get a free trip to Greece, Bali, or the Indian subcontinent.

13. Kaleidoscopes from the 1950s. They were wonderful; we remember terrible fights with our kids because we wanted to look first. Search your attics, local flea markets, and tag sales.

14. Memorabilia from famous stores that have gone out of business. Examples are DePinna, Best & Co, and McCutcheon & Plummer.

Since these stores were a great shopping attraction for two earlier generations of shoppers, you ought to ransack family attics to see if there are any bags, catalogs, boxes, advertising posters, or sale announcements left from them.

15. Motorcycle paper goods. Magazines, posters, and other related items—keep anything relating to motorcycles.

16. Painter hats. Those worn by adolescents, with logos from stores known to no more than fifty customers or which say things like "Salta PVC Pipe Lining."

17. Paintings by little-known American artists. How do you find them if they are little-known? Study Groce and Wallace's *The New York Historical Society's Dictionary of American Artists* and choose a painter who is only mentioned once.

18. Early Stanley tools. Look at your screwdriver and you'll see why; they are beautifully made.

19. Sterling silver Georgian nipple shields from the late eighteenth century. They run around $300 and will go up.

20. Marlo Thomas dolls. If you see one, buy it even if the price tag is $400. They are rare and will appreciate.

21. WPA art. The Works Progress Administration was the New Deal's program that subsidized artists, theater people, and writers during the Depression.

The Federal Art Project employed 3,600 people—easel painters, graphic artists, and muralists. Thousands of paintings, prints, and posters were created but most have been lost. Recent renewed interest in the WPA, however, has produced events like the 1977 WPA art exhibition at the Parsons School of Design in New York City. We think the catalog of that show, *New York City WPA Art,* is a future collectible, as is the already rare history of the Federal Theatre Project, *Free, Adult, Uncensored.*

The Federal Writers' Project produced many guide books, some of which, like the *The WPA Guide to New York City,* have been reissued. We predict that both the originals and the reissues will become collector's items.

The WPA was a regional project with centers in New York City, Cleveland, Chicago, San Francisco, and Philadelphia. Bits and pieces of WPA art and crafts surface from time to time. All of it will become more valuable. Be on the lookout for paintings, prints, and posters by WPA artists; composition and rag dolls; toys, examples of weaving, metal work, and wood carving; and early American furniture reproductions made in WPA craft shops, particularly in Illinois.

The Philadelphia Museum of Art has the largest collection of WPA prints and posters in the country but it is, unfortunately, not exhibited. The Library of Congress maintains a research facility for scholars interested in the WPA.

22. Wedding cake tops. Our friend, Roberta Dixon, started to collect these objects after her daughter's wedding, for which the caterer produced a cake top that was "pure plastic tacky, hideous but consciousness raising." She began to buy them at tag sales, usually for a quarter, and now has more than forty in her collection. The best are the early ones, produced before plastic took over in 1965. They are made of bisque and plaster of Paris and go back to 1910. Roberta has tops made of pairs of bells, but most feature painted figures of brides and grooms, examples of simple folk craft. You can tell the period by the clothing, which shows changes in style, and by the hairdos. For example, the pre-flapper of 1918 wore body-fitting dresses and hair that was cropped close to her head.

Prices have already gone up; Dixon says that she has to pay $15 for a good bisque top today because they are getting scarce. We don't mean to make her life difficult with this prediction, but we think wedding cake tops will be sought after collectibles and that prices will escalate.

Choice Tips

In choosing items that are likely to become the collectibles of the future, look for:

Beauty and Style. For example, hand made sterling silver jewelry, especially pieces signed by the maker.

Logos. Anything that carries a famous company's logo, such as a toy truck or car, or an "I Love My Cat" magnetic pad and pen will become collectible.

The trick is to order at least three of any item you choose to collect—one for your youngster to play with, a second to lock away unopened in the attic, and the third one to replace the one you have hidden, which your child will find and destroy. (We suggest that serious collectors leave the extras in some other house—not Grandma's, because she'll give them to the kids the minute they beg, but someone you can trust who lives far away. The shipping may get expensive, but your collectibles will be safe.)

History. Study the collectibles of the past. They are valuable not only because they are rare, but also because they tell us something about other periods of our history. American kids of the Depression loved the Lone Ranger and Little Orphan Annie because these radio shows were often the only moments of cheer in a life that was otherwise a continuous struggle.

Right now, for example, mail-order catalogs are big business and we think that some of them are coming collectibles. Send for every free one you see, on the chance that it may be beautiful or tell an important story. Remember that historians, museum curators, and antique dealers use them to authenticate what was available in the past. You can study the advertisements of organizations that sell catalogs—some of them are stunning and, like posters, will increase in value. You just have to decide which ones.

Watch Your F's and K's

In case you are confused about how much you should learn before starting to collect, here is our favorite ignorance-isn't-bliss story.

Tag sale colleagues of ours were excited to find an Audubon folio they knew was valuable at a small sale they were running in Massachusetts. They called their book dealer to authenticate it. When he came, he immediately offered them $2,500. They were overjoyed. He promised to return the next day to pick it up. But, when he opened it to examine it once more, he was incensed. During the night someone had carefully cut out the flyleaf, which contained the date of the edition, making the folio absolutely worthless. Our friends were bewildered until they discovered that the owner was the culprit. Her late husband's name was written on the flyleaf and she did not want anyone to know she was selling her personal possessions.

Be careful with jewelry as well. We have a cousin who had a ring sized recently. When she got it back from the jewelry shop, she was horrified to find they had excised part of the word "Tiffany," and the "1" from the "14 Karat," making this expensive item much less valuable. You must watch out for all your K's!

Another warning—don't believe everything you read. An advertisement appearing in the "Swap Box" column of the magazine *Collectibles Illustrated,* offered to exchange an old MG convertible for a Currier & Ives original. A friend was ready to write when we warned her that her Currier & Ives is too badly spotted and stained; it will not even get her a tricycle.

Now that you know something about collecting, you are probably curious to learn what the things you have bought or inherited may be worth. You can start reading, taking courses, doing research. But there is an easier way—you can have your possessions appraised. How do you go about this? Don't worry, it's right here. All you have to do is turn the page.

F & S's Quick Tips

- **TRUST YOUR OWN TASTE AND INSTINCTS**
- **BUY WHAT YOU LOVE**
- **BUY THE BEST EXAMPLES OF WHATEVER YOU ARE COLLECTING**

3

Appraisals: If You Broke Your Arm, Would You Set It Yourself?

Of course not. You'd take it to an orthopedic surgeon. So, if you want to know what Grandma's antique jewelry is really worth, you need an expert opinion.

For example, almost everyone of our clients thinks they have a blanket chest that came over on the Mayflower. If all of the blanket chests for which such claims are made were really authentic, the Mayflower would have sunk long before it ever got to America. We have never appraised one that actually arrived with the Pilgrims. The garden-variety blanket chests we most often see are late nineteenth- or early twentieth-century maple, a wood that did not even exist in England of the 1620s.

It is not much fun destroying people's illusions, but often we must. Recently we were appraising the contents of a home outside of Boston. We kept hearing, while we were still on the first floor, of the "very old" partners' desk in "my husband's study upstairs." For those of you unfortunate enough never to have seen one, this partners' desk was a large mahogany piece, perhaps thirty-one inches high by five feet wide by four and a half feet deep, having a flat top with banded inlay and a center drawer, flanked on each side by drawers. The partners sit facing each other.

Partners' desks are relatively rare. This one had descended from the husband's ancestors and was his favorite piece in a house crammed with lovely things. We had to tell him it wasn't a partners' desk at all. It was an early twentieth-century sideboard in the Federal style whose legs had been preemptively cut down.

Fine Arts Insurance Appraisal

There are many different kinds of appraisals. One of the most common is for fine arts insurance coverage, which includes your antiques, silver, china, crystal, Oriental rugs, jewelry, and other valuables. This type of appraisal establishes the current replacement value, that is, what it would cost to purchase an early twentieth-century French Longwy pottery lamp if you were lucky enough to find one, should yours be stolen or melted down in a fire. Even if you cannot locate another or a similar lamp, you are entitled to receive the amount it was worth from your insurance company, but only if you have a written appraisal. If you don't have a separate fine arts listing, you may have to prove that you owned the piece and you may only receive the amount you paid for it, rather than its actual replacement value. Since inflation and the tides of collecting can cause rapid alterations in the market, an insurance appraisal should be updated every three to five years.

The absence of fine arts insurance coverage can be costly because most homeowners' policies have a whole series of exclusions. No matter what the overall allowance for the contents of your home, whether $30,000 or $150,000, each policy states the amount that covers specific categories. Generally it is $1,000 for sterling silver, $250 for furs and jewelry, $500 for securities, and $3,000 for your new computer, should these items be stolen or destroyed. These days you can get a fur button and one quarter of a watch for $250. To discover the particulars of your policy, try reading it. While it is not *Fanny Hill*, it will be vastly educational regarding the protection you actually have.

Ignorance Is Not Bliss; It Is Costly

This is what can happen to people who do not read their policies, stubbornly refuse to buy and read this book, fail to have their valuables appraised, and leave their suburban houses unoccupied during the summer. Friends of ours, who live in Connecticut and have a vacation home on Nantucket, installed a burglar alarm and an elaborate timing mechanism to turn the lights on and off in their Connecticut home. They registered with the police department's "empty house" list, asked their neighbors to keep an eye on their property and call the authorities if anyone arrived with a truck and started removing everything they owned. Then they went off to eat lobster and play tennis all summer.

But thieves are sophisticated these days—they know how to dismantle alarms, identify timers which, unlike real people, turn the living room lights off at exactly the same moment every night, and figure out when the neighbors will not be looking (around 3 A.M. Even unsophisticated thieves can figure that out.). So naturally our friends' flatware was stolen, along with a small TV, two portable radios, an antique Oriental throw rug in the foyer and whatever jewelry the thieves could find. It was a neat job—a quick cut of the alarm wires, a pane of glass removed in the dining room and zingo. The burglary was not discovered until the youngster who watered the house plants every week arrived and wondered about the broken window and the open drawer in the dining room sideboard.

Our friends thought they had adequate coverage, until they called their insurance agent and discovered the $1,000 limit on sterling. When they started shopping, they were appalled. The silver inflation had passed its zenith, but a new set just like the one they had owned cost $5,000.

Says the wife, with resignation, "So now we are eating with stainless. At first I was rather pleased. I found this very smart modern set and thought about how I'd never polish silver again. After all, Americans are too materialistic, everyone says so. That baloney lasted until I gave our first postrobbery dinner party. I set the table and it was like one of those dishwasher ads on TV that blink, signifying what a wonderful job a particular dishwasher soap will do with your glassware. Well, I looked, or rather, I fixated. There was the gold and white Lenox I had inherited from Mother, the Waterford crystal we received as wedding gifts, and there was that damn modern stainless blinking away, announcing the theft all over again. I stopped lying to myself that it didn't matter and have been borrowing my neighbor's sterling when I entertain ever since. As soon as I save up enough to replace it, I am going to take my own private appraiser (OPA) along and put her to work immediately."

We hope she chooses carefully; OPAs may become collectible.

When Your Valuables Wander

If your kids or your neighbors want to borrow sterling or other portable valuables, you can relax. Your insurance will cover your property even if it is stolen from the folks next door or your daughter's house. However, if you rent your home, you must let your insurance company know and rearrange your coverage according to the new situation. Insurance companies, when they write a fine arts policy, assume your valuables will be under your care. If they are not, your agent will advise you on what to do.

One of our more generous clients gave a number of extremely valuable sterling silver objects to her only daughter, who left them tarnishing in the kitchen until they were stolen by an obliging thief who didn't mind how dirty they were. The young woman had not bothered with fine arts insurance and was unable to collect enough money from her homeowner's policy to begin to replace them.

Her mother, who had been planning to give her the flatware as well, changed her mind. A wise move, since it happened to be Tiffany's finest heavy weight silver in the Chrysanthemum pattern. It was the most complete silver service we have ever appraised, stored in a fitted box specially made by Tiffany to accommodate the entire set. We put a replacement value of $22,000 on this service. Without our appraisal and the fine arts insurance policy our client quickly bought, all she would have collected, had the set been nabbed, was that famous $1,000, plus several buckets full of tears.

Easing Disaster

And then there was Aunt Ethel and the oak tree. Aunt Ethel is our favorite, a dear, disheveled, slender woman who dotes on disaster. She's the one who reads the obituaries every day and goes through the airplane crashes, house fires, local robberies, and major murders like a miser pouring over stock market tables. We've always assumed it was because nothing exciting had happened to Aunt Ethel in years.

One August morning, though, she called us in a state of ardent hysteria, mumbling about the tea service and the cherry table. We rushed over to find that the previous night's storm had blown down her neighbor's oak tree, which had landed on the sun porch roof, shattering a portion of it and causing considerable damage to the walls and windows. The fact that it was raining inside her house, and had been all night, didn't trouble Aunt Ethel; it was the crushed and battered state of the lovely old cherry dropleaf table she'd inherited from her mother, and the disfiguring dents and scratches in the sterling silver tea service that had stood on top of it, which were driving her mad.

We gently reminded her that everything was insured. She brightened as she recalled the appraisal we had done two years before. Her neighbors were so concerned about the damage their tree had caused that they insisted on taking care of hiring contractors to fix the house. Meanwhile, Aunt Ethel made plans to find replacements.

Appraisal Surprises

An eighty-year-old Judge called us in grudgingly; he didn't really want to spend the money for an appraisal but was forced to do so by his insurance company. His agent had informed him that the company had refused to renew his homeowner's policy without a documented fine arts appraisal of his sterling and paintings.

It was his own fault. For years he had been claiming that the paintings were worth a bloody fortune. One of these was a 1930s full-length portrait of his first wife in the style of John Singer Sargent, which was still hanging over the nuptial bed despite the presence of a second wife. Whether this was more or less disturbing to her than a vial of ashes on the living room mantel would have been, we never established.

There were a lot of paintings all right, but they were primarily of religious subjects, with spectacularly little commercial market value. We have nothing against religious paintings; it's just that, like cows, they don't sell.*

---

* Actually, cows may be making a comeback. Last year, a smashing oil depicting eight of them, by the English Victorian painter Thomas Sidney Cooper, brought £6,500 at a Phillips auction in London. And oxen are really in. Richard Bourne Galleries in Hyannis, Massachusetts, brought down the hammer at $9,500 for an oil by Robert D. Wilkie, the 19th Century American painter, featuring a gorgeous pair of them pulling an ox-cart.

It was not much fun relaying this news. The client was upset and, for a while, we thought the appraisal was over before it had really begun. But he was restored to good humor and joy when we noticed four plaques hanging high on the kitchen wall. Climbing gingerly up an antique stepladder to get them, we saw that they were early twentieth-century Quimper faience pieces from Brittany, purchased for $3 each thirty years ago, but worth $350 a piece today. We tried hard not to drop them while putting them back.

As so often happens, surprises being an integral part of all appraising, we found other treasures the judge had no idea he owned. There was a well-preserved crocodile medical bag which had belonged to his physician father, who probably paid no more than $20 for it at the turn of the century. It would cost about three hundred 1985 dollars. The lamps, china, rugs, and some of the furniture also turned out to be valuable. By the end of the appraisal he was delighted, lovingly patting his now worthy tables and chairs, and singing the praises of his insurance agent, of us, and of the glories of inflation. The paintings had been forgotten.

Alarms and Appraisals

Most people do not wait until the insurance company forces them to have their worldly goods appraised so that they can get fine arts insurance coverage. Between 1973 and 1981, stolen property in New York City alone rose from $283,000,000 to $954,000,000, according to the New York City Police Department; for the nation as a whole, theft runs into the billions of dollars. Ordinary citizens are aware of this unfortunate trend, causing the market in burglar alarms and guard dogs to soar. The items most often stolen are those which are portable, from clothing and airline tickets to gold necklaces, sterling silver and Tiffany pins. The only way to recover the real market value of the latter three items is to have them evaluated by a recognized appraiser and recorded for all time in an appraisal report.

In the long run, an appraisal is probably cheaper, and definitely less messy, than installing and maintaining an alarm system or feeding the dog for fourteen years. And you can't cut the wires on an appraiser or easily poison her/him the way you can, respectively, an electronic system or an animal.

Not only do insurance companies require a fine arts appraisal for proper coverage of your valuables, but common sense dictates it. Most people cannot recreate or even describe what is in their living or dining rooms before fire destroys them, much less remember after the shock of loss. Nor can they assign a current market value to that "thing-a-ma-jig of Grandpa's with the ebony handle and silver screw," which happened to be an antique, English roast bone-holder. Imagine, then, how difficult it would be for your relatives and heirs, who visit your home once a year at Christmas, to reconstruct your possessions, should you die suddenly in an accident, or from an illness, the very same week your house burns down or thieves decide to loot it because it is empty.

Even if you have photographs or videotapes of your belongings, they do not show the exact size of an object, the material from which it is made, the condition it is in, or if any part of it has been replaced, all of which affect its value. Bills of sale are of little use because that English mahogany gateleg table you bought in the sixties is worth at least three to four times more today than what you paid for it, unless you were horribly gypped. Besides, a photograph could have been taken next door, or at your Aunt Jane's. By itself, without a bill of sale, it may prove you are a terrific photographer, but not that you actually owned the piece.

Thus, if your possessions include European or American antiques, sterling silver flatware or hollowware, paintings and/or lithographs by recognized artists, fine china and/or crystal, valuable lamps, old Oriental rugs, gold, silver, or antique jewelry, pewter or any of the other odds and ends one finds in antique shops, auction houses and, occasionally, at garage, yard, and tag sales, you should have those items professionally appraised.

It is true that an appraisal cannot replace a damaged or destroyed work of art or the pearl necklace and gold bracelets stolen while you were on vacation. Nor can it ease the pain and sense of outrage we all feel when we are robbed. But it will give you the necessary insurance protection to reduce or eliminate the financial loss.

What Insurance Can (and Cannot) Do

Some people even make money when appraised goods are stolen. At the height of the silver boom, burglaries occurred in epidemic proportions throughout suburban areas. Homeowners responded by ordering appraisals en masse; there was one month when we were thinking of establishing a fire sale appraisal rate. One of our clients had her considerable silver collection valued at that time; her sterling flatware was stolen two years later. A few months before the theft the market had dropped, but our client collected on the basis of what was written in the appraisal and made a small fortune. She was able to replace the silver and take a cruise. It was not that she got something for nothing. She had paid for the appraisal and for the policy. It was more like winning a lottery.

However, and it is a big one, this is not the usual situation; it happened only because she owned an antique set of sterling that was irreplaceable. The client had to be satisfied with silver that resembled hers, but cost less.

The theory behind insurance is to make you whole again after you have suffered a loss, but not to make you more than whole. Your insurance company is not going to send you to Aruba. Even with fine arts coverage, they will pay you the current market value of any items in your appraisal that are still available. Thus, if you own Gorham's Sovereign pattern, and the company still makes it, you will receive a settlement to cover the actual replacement cost of that particular set. However, with unique items that are no longer manufactured, you get the amount written in the appraisal, since that is the only standard the company has in determining your loss.

Resale Appraisal

Another reason to call in appraisers is the desire to sell some of your property to make way for new purchases, provide some much needed cash, or just because you can't stand looking at it anymore. This kind of appraisal can be verbal or written and provides you with the market value of your possessions, what they will bring if you decide to put them into a tag sale or sell them at auction, to a dealer, or to your friends down the block.

Why not just ask the dealer what they are worth? Because a wise man or woman learns the value of an article from a person who has nothing whatever to do with its sale.

Where we appraise the contents of a house and then are asked to handle the sale, we never charge for the appraisal, only for the sale. Under no circumstances should appraisers have a financial interest in selling the merchandise they are valuing.

Basement Bonanzas

Resale appraisals are also full of surprises. Recently we were called in to value some of the contents of a New Jersey home. The family wished to sell their painted living and dining room furniture, upholstered chairs, assorted tables, broken sets of dishes, even a cracked crockpot. We had to tell them that everything was unsalable because of the poor condition of the items, and we recommended that they give it to their children or donate the lot to charity. The only item of any real value they had was a beautifully preserved, square rattan table hidden under a gray flannel cover in the den.

It took us a mere fifteen minutes to give our opinion, and we were getting ready to leave, chalking up another absent fee, when the lady of the house said, "That table is really worth something?"

"You bet it is."

"Oh," she said, smiling, "I have more in the basement. We hate it."

"Let's see," we murmured.

Downstairs, we found the entire set, including a settee, a chaise, two armchairs, and two more tables like the one we had already seen. All the upholstered pieces were covered in the original fabric, a crisp green cotton printed with ocean liners. The set had been manufactured in the 1930s and was in mint condition.

"You really want to sell this?" we asked.

The family nodded in unison.

"Well, it is worth at least $3,000. In Greenwich, Connecticut, or on the upper west side of New York City, there are people who would kill for it. A similar set sold at auction in Bolton, Massachusetts, for $3500 this year, and if any California collectors knew it was here, they would be camping on your doorstep."

While they were sputtering, "You're kidding," and "Oh, my God," we noticed, on the floor next to the settee, a stuffed swordfish four-and-a-half-feet long, which the lady of the house said she was either going to throw out or give back to her first husband.

"Don't," we cried, "you can get $250 to $300 for it. We know someone who lost one just like it at auction recently. He is still mumbling, 'You should have seen the one that got away.' "

By this time we were going through the basement with microscopic precision. In the corner, half hidden behind some plywood boards, we discovered a 1940s jukebox which played 78rpm records. It had been there since the family moved in and had stood undisturbed because they never got around to giving it away.

"Good thing, too," we said. "It's worth in the neighborhood of $2,500, but only because it is not in top condition. Otherwise, you could get much more."

Now that we were clearly earning our fee, we sat down with the family and outlined the possible options for handling these valuables. They could decide to keep them, waiting for them to be worth even more, or enjoy them because the outside world had decreed their substantive value. They could donate them to charity and claim a handsome tax deduction, but only with a written appraisal, which is required by the IRS. They could give them to their grown children, who occasionally deserve something more than chipped crockery and bent spoons. They could call in a furniture dealer to sell the rattan set and know precisely what to ask for it. They could even hire us to include the items in our next house sale. Of course, if that happened, the cost of the appraisal would be applied to the sale commission.

Consultant Services

Sometimes we tell clients that it doesn't pay for them to hire us, that what they intend to sell is worth so little, the proceeds would not cover the overhead and our commission.

Recently a woman, who was moving to Florida, decided to sell everything in her apartment rather than ship it south. For a consultant's fee, we went over her belongings, helped her price them, taught her how to place them so that they would show to the greatest advantage, advised her to shine the silver, vacuum the rugs, and go over all the wood pieces with scratch cover. We told her where to advertise, how to write the ad and what to say, including directions to her apartment; indicated the best days and hours to hold the sale; went over such matters as crowd control, signs, the sales help she would need; how to write sales checks and keep records for tax purposes; and how to provide lunch for an all-day sale. Finally, we reminded her to get money from the bank so that she would be able to make change. For the rare occasions when you should do it yourself see Section Two, Part Three, The Reluctant F&S Guide to Running Your Own House Sale.

Estate Appraisal

Then there is the estate appraisal. You may think it means the Du Ponts want us and all our financial worries are forever over. Unfortunately, the "estate" in this case refers to the deceased. This appraisal seeks to establish the lowest possible realistic value to avoid overpaying inheritance taxes.

Recently we were hired by a family of elderly heirs to appraise the contents of their mother's Lake Shore Drive apartment. Mom had died six months before but the heirs were still tiptoeing around, and nothing, not even a lace doily, was out of place. We found a wonderful French Art Deco* sterling silver tea set with ivory mounts, which we valued at $3,000. We also told our clients that it would bring between $5,000 and $9,000 if they decided to sell it, and that, for insurance purposes, it would cost $18,000 to replace it. This gives you some idea how the same object can have many different numbers legitimately attached to it, and how the types of appraisals run into each other.

Appraising and Advising

For example, we were called by a troubled young couple after the husband's grandmother died. He was deeply grieved and simply could not deal with her apartment; he wanted us to live up to our motto and "make everything go away." But his wife liked some of the things and thought he'd be glad to have them when he got over his despair.

* 1920s to the early 1930s

We did an estate appraisal. Grandmother had never thrown away a thing. Rag pickers that we are, we started with the mountain of textiles that had been assembled in the dining room—clothing, linens, curtains going back fifty years. The most valuable item here turned out to be an eighteenth-century embroidered silk bell pull worth $200, because it was only in fair condition—had it been well preserved it would have brought much more.

Our young client was impressed that she could realize that much money from something she had thought to be absolutely worthless, and suggested we guide her about what she should keep, sell, or give away. She ended up with almost $10,000 by selling an eighteenth-century French commode with a marble top for $7,500; a Hutschenreuther Art Deco porcelain figurine for $200; rococo andirons of Doré bronze, which brought $350; and a collection of vintage nineteenth-century handbags, some known as reticules, worth about $1,800.

Meanwhile she kept the Renaissance Revival banquet size dining table and chairs, and a set of Sinclair American engraved crystal stemware, circa 1910, which would have brought $300 had she chosen to sell it. What she did sell was a less valuable gold-banded set of crystal stemware from the same period for $75.

Appraising and Arbitrating

Appraisers are most valuable when they serve as arbitrators and are able to give unbiased advice to feuding families. A lawyer hired us to value the contents of a recently deceased couple's apartment because the heirs, a son and two daughters, were quarreling. It seemed that the son, who was the executor of his parents' estate, claimed that their total belongings were worth only $3,000. The sisters became suspicious that he was undervaluing their possessions so that he could keep them himself. They rebelled and insisted on an appraisal.

They were right. We took one look at the early nineteenth-century French mahogany *bonheur du jour* (a ladies writing desk), inlaid with satinwood and gilt mounts, and knew it alone was worth $2,000 to $3,000. A Victorian dresser set, complete with ring tree and dresser jars, which he had said was silverplate, turned out to be sterling, and would bring $450 on the open market, though we valued it at $200 for estate purposes. But then we were puzzled—there was no sterling silver flatware, no dishes. The brother maintained there had been none, but it was clear the parents had not been eating with their hands or off paper plates.

Reluctantly he led us to the sideboard, where we found the sterling. Later we located the dishes, stored in zippered plastic protectors in the highest kitchen cabinets, the ones usually reserved for picnic baskets, citronella lamps, and other seasonal items used only rarely.

Seeing that these siblings were as likely to agree on how to divide their parents' possessions as Britain and Argentina would be over who should keep the Falkland Islands, our advice was to sell everything. Money is easy to divide. Which is how an estate appraisal can turn into a division appraisal.

Division Appraisal

A division appraisal is done in cases of divorce or inheritance, where clients have to parcel out property, and must know the relative value of every piece at issue. A division appraisal is a resale value appraisal, that is, the wholesale price, or what a dealer will offer for it.

We have a very grateful client in Denver, Colorado, a successful businessman who had separated from his wife and gotten into a hassle over the financial settlement. Since they had three children, who were living with their mother, he was sending a generous monthly allowance for their care. He became concerned because, every time he visited the youngsters, he saw they had nothing. What was she doing with the money?

He and his lawyer wondered if she was using it to buy antique furniture and paintings for the designer dress boutique she was planning to open. We were hired to appraise these valuable items, which turned out to be worth $75,000. This special form of division appraisal gave the husband information on which he could base a fair and equitable offer. They settled out of court.

Appraise First, Move Later

The case of a brother and sister from Philadelphia illustrates an important point. These two had shared the cost of having all of their mother's furniture shipped from California so that they could divide it fairly, only to discover it was used furniture, with little resale value, not a load of precious and irreplaceable antiques, as Mother had always claimed. The moral of that story is to appraise before storing or shipping. How could they have found an appraiser long distance? They could have bought this book and read Chapter Four. Which is what you must do to get the same information.

Generous Grandmother

Then there was the lady from Harrison, New York, who had been living for the last thirty years in a fifteen-room center-hall colonial complete with gray shingles, white shutters, and roses growing over a picket fence. It got to be too much for her and she decided to move into a small apartment in a retirement village. She took her favorite furniture with her, and asked her daughter and daughter-in-law to find out what everything else was worth, so that her possessions could be divided between their two families, which included several grown grandchildren. We appraised the entire lot, describing each piece. We won't print the whole thing here, only a few items to give you an idea of what kind of information was included in her division appraisal report.

Here are some items from her dining room. (All measurements are in height, width and depth.)

Early twentieth-century American mahogany dining table having double shaped pedestal extending to quadruped base terminating in cast brass paw feet
28″ × 12′ × 47″ $900

Early nineteenth-century English mahogany butler's chest of four drawers having slightly shaped front
30″ × 29″ × 16″ $1,000

Set of eight early twentieth-century American mahogany side chairs in Chippendale style having leather upholstered seats with ribbon backs $600/8

Late nineteenth-century European majolica planter in the form of
a shoe encrusted with flowers, some chips $35

Late nineteenth-century Fradley sterling silver water pitcher with
cast handle, some dents $250

In our opinion, the dents considerably reduced the value of the
pitcher and we advised having it repaired. We gave our clients the
names of two local shops which do excellent work, and price guidelines
regarding what such a repair would cost.*

The two daughters were delighted and persuaded their mother to
have us appraise the pieces she had taken with her. Our appraisal ratified
the authenticity of her possessions and gave her children some idea of
what would be coming to them in the future. Naturally, the value of
their mother's things would have to be updated at the time they were
actually divided.

Gift Appraisals

Say you have ordered a division appraisal and have actually
apportioned everything wanted by the heirs. There are still those items
no one wants. You collectively decide to give all the old books to the
historical society, the clothing, kitchen utensils, and used furniture to a
social service or religious organization, and the old hats and handbags to
the high school drama club to adorn its period plays for the next decade.
If you want to take advantage of the tax deduction that you can claim,
only an appraiser can establish a value of each donated item that will
satisfy the IRS. Even the opinion of your local historical society will not
be accepted by the tax men.

Giving Away Is Not Easy

One of our particular services is finding obscure charities which
will take things no one else wants. (No, we don't give out that list—do

---

* If you need information about restorers and conservators, call the nearest museum
or historical society. They should be able to direct you to reliable artisans.

great chefs tell you how they make a mousse?) Another is that we are absurdly honest. Once we were called to a beautifully-appointed estate to dispose of the junk. On a Ping-Pong table in the basement there it all stood—the plastic margarine containers, tin pie plates, assorted pot tops, dusty, twisted, unkempt foreign dolls, and those little glasses in which they pack prepared shrimp cocktail. We told the owner there was no selling this stuff; they could try giving it away, or they could lug it to the town dump. (This was an absurd suggestion because these people didn't even know there was a town dump.) But one item intrigued us—an ancient car battery so old that its fluid had leaked all over the place. We lifted it up and discovered that it had been resting on a tray which was blackened and deeply corroded from the battery acid. We recognized an early Tiffany mark on the back, had it professionally polished down to another layer, and then sold it for $750. We collected our twenty-percent commission and the client got the rest.

Documents

No matter what kind of appraisal you need, there is a certain amount of paperwork involved, fortunately for the appraiser, not for you.

The first document you should receive is a contract, which will state the kind of appraisal you have ordered; the hourly rate or flat fee for the service and what it covers, normally the time in your home plus off-site hours spent on research and the preparation of the appraisal report; how much of a deposit is required and when it is due; when the report will be presented, and when final payment is expected.

Then, within a couple of weeks of the appraiser's visit, you should receive at least two copies of the appraisal report, which will include all the items you had the appraiser value, listed room by room, as in the example above. Some clients prefer to have their possessions listed by category or collection. We are pleased to do this, but it is considerably more expensive because it takes more time to organize.

The first page of the appraisal report should include:

1. The date and type of the appraisal.

2. The various categories of your possessions, such as fine arts objects, which are paintings, rugs, and furniture; breakable fine arts, such as china and crystal; and sterling silver and jewelry.

3. The value of each category, for example, $18,000 worth of silver, plus the overall total value.

4. A statement that all items are in good condition unless otherwise indicated.

5. The sequence of measurements, such as H = height, W = width, L = length, D = depth, and Dia. = diameter.

6. An explanation of any abbreviations used, like FAB to indicate fine arts breakable, SS for sterling silver, J for jewelry and FA for fine arts (antiques and paintings).

7. An explanation that the term "style" means that the article is not "of the period" but is a later copy or reproduction.

8. A statement that the appraisers have no financial interest in the items appraised and do not contemplate any such interest in the future.

Those of us who are compulsive appraisers even include the number of pages in the report, in case one gets inadvertently lost. Naturally, page one should be signed by the appraisers.

If you order an appraisal because you are going to buy fine arts insurance, shop around for your policy. This area of the insurance business is in flux, and policies and prices differ. The important points for you to know are:

1. There are two types of fine arts insurance—commercial, for galleries and museums, and private, for individual collectors.

2. Fortunately for you, the cost of private fine arts insurance is less than for commercial policies because gallery and museum art is more likely to be moved around for exhibitions and is therefore at a greater risk of being damaged or stolen.

3. Insurance brokers are willing to customize policies to meet the needs of individual clients.

4. The field is highly competitive and premiums for private fine arts insurance vary. Get several quotes. This is where the summary information on the first page of your appraisal comes in handy because it contains the totals for each category, for example, $24,000 worth of fine arts objects, $13,000 of breakable fine arts objects, and $20,000 worth of silver. With this, you can do your comparison shopping by phone.

5. The heart of any fine arts policy is the "valuation clause," which sets out how you will be compensated in case of loss. That is why it is important to keep track of changes in the worth of your possessions through updated appraisals, unless you choose an "agreed amount" valuations clause, which specifies how much you will get before a loss occurs.

6. Security plays a role in obtaining fine arts insurance. Brokers tend to inquire if you have a burglar and/or fire alarm. While insurance agents, with their eyes constantly on the competition, are currently loath to require these protections, if company and industry losses are great, they may do so in the future.

7. There are companies that specialize, or do over fifty percent of their business, in the fine arts field.*

Everyone thinks fine arts insurance is prohibitive, but it is not. One of our clients insured $23,000 worth of silver for $137 and just under $40,000 worth of fine arts objects for $73 in 1984, for a total annual cost of $210.

After you have selected an insurance company, one copy of the appraisal report goes to it; the other should find its way to your safe-deposit box in a hurry so that, if your house burns down, the appraisal won't go with it. Burnt up appraisals are absolutely useless.

The average cost for a good appraiser runs from $50 to $175 an hour—one of the major New York City auction houses charges $1000 a day. The cost of a fine arts appraisal for a seven room house should run somewhere between $800 and $1500. The appraiser should always charge a flat fee or hourly rate, never a percentage; the latter is considered

* For more information, see page 91 of the October 1984 issue of *Art & Auction* for an article on fine arts insurance.

unethical because the tendency then is to overvalue the goods. We advise pushing for the flat fee if you hire an excellent but slow-moving appraiser.

When we say "good," we mean be careful. There are no overall standards for appraisers and no licensing. Anyone can have cards printed, put an ad in the yellow pages, and be in business, though how long uninformed appraisers remain self-employed is another question.

How do you find such a person—one who is honest, well-trained and reliable? Can one appraiser tell what all of your valuables including your silver, china, crystal, and antique English furniture are worth? Do they call in experts when, and if, they are not sure? Isn't that a lot of money, just to find out that you have to pay yet another insurance premium?

The methods of locating and appraising the appraiser are waiting for you in Chapter Four. But be forewarned—this is just the first of many areas about which you must learn if you have the fortune to own articles of value or intend to acquire them.

There are two important elements at work here. One is the Compulsion to Own Syndrome and the other is the Compulsion to Own in a Hurry Syndrome. They should be mutually exclusive but they are not. This is a subject you will hear about until you are sick of it as you go through this book. But it cannot be emphasized strongly enough. If you buy without knowledge, it will cost you a lot of money and aggravation. Acquisitive people must take the time to learn.

For example, we know of a couple who took a family vacation in St. Croix in 1968. The father of this family has always been a restless individual with the soul of a collector. One day he disappeared. Five hours later he returned with five Tekke Oriental carpets in the familiar field pattern, ranging in size from throw to room.

"I found an auction," he admitted sheepishly.

"In St. Croix?" asked his incredulous wife. "Who auctions rugs in the Virgin Islands?"

"They were a fabulous buy," he insisted, "Don't complain."

When the family appeared at the airport, with the five neatly rolled and tied Oriental rugs, the baggage clerk was noticeably agitated. Would the big carpets break his scale? Where in his rule book did it say he had to transport them?

Our friends stared him down. "We never travel without them," said the father sternly.

Back in New York, his wife made a few inquiries and discovered her husband had overpaid only mildly for carpets readily available, and on sale that very week, at B. Altman & Company.

This kind of experience, which is not particularly unique, is the reason we cannot help but admire the behavior, which some might consider tactless, of the medic in our favorite appraisal story.

One rainy day last summer, Jeri was on her way to an antiques show in Chicago, driving with associates in their van. The driver made a sudden turn, the van skidded, and flipped over twice. Jeri was injured.

When the ambulance arrived, the attendants wanted to know what she was doing there, where they were going, and how the accident had occurred. She was, by this time, flat on her back on a stretcher, being carried toward the ambulance and moaning. Wearily, she explained that they were on their way to an antiques show and that she is an appraiser.

"Oh," said the physician on call, smiling down at her, "my wife and I, we have this little Carnival glass bowl," he went on, cupping his hands into the shape of his bowl. "If I describe it, could you tell me what it is worth?"

F & S's Quick Tips

- IGNORANCE IS COSTLY: HAVE YOUR VALUABLES APPRAISED
- THEFT IS LIKELY: PROTECT YOURSELF
- APPRAISERS ARE MULTIFUNCTIONAL: THEY VALUE, ADVISE, CONSULT, AND ARBITRATE
- FINE ARTS INSURANCE IS ESSENTIAL

Chapter 4

Possession May Be Nine-Tenths of the Law, But Organization Is What Saves Money

Or, How To: Find an Appraiser   Appraise the Appraiser   Organize for an Appraisal

Okay, another neighbor was robbed last week and is crying about being underinsured. You've decided to find out how much your worldly goods are really worth before it happens to you.

You are about to save a lot of money by spending it. How? Just one minor loss, say the disappearance of two sterling serving platters and assorted knives and forks, which can easily be lifted during a dinner party, or by a speedy thief in the middle of the night, and you have paid for the appraisal.

Finding an Appraiser

Here are some tested procedures for locating a reliable appraiser. After all, you can't let just anyone into your home. Even utility company meter readers, vacuum cleaner salespersons, evangelists bringing God to your doorstep, and those relentless little nymphs selling Girl Scout cookies have to be scrutinized with care these days.

First, make a list of appraisers to interview in your locality. A good place to start collecting information about such people is from the professional organizations in this field. The largest are the American Society of Appraisers (ASA), the Appraisers Association of America, and the International Society of Appraisers. They all publish directories which list their memberships by location and areas of expertise.*

These groups represent a wide range of appraisal specialists and provide you with some protection because they have standards for membership. You can't just pay a fee and join; you have to know something. In fact, ASA recommends that you find out what qualifications the appraiser you are thinking of hiring has demonstrated. For example, is she/he allowed to display a professional symbol, similar to the ASA designation its tested and certified members may use? This title signifies that ASA appraisers have passed a written examination; have had at least five years of appraisal experience; have presented representative appraisal reports; and have been screened regarding the ethical standards under which they operate. Similarly, the International Society of Appraisers requires five years of experience before one can become a member.

These societies also have entry level or associate designation for appraisers who are in the process of becoming fully accredited. Associates are usually more than competent to value your possessions. Just as you don't need the professor of surgery for your routine appendectomy, you do not require the national expert on early nineteenth-century American furniture to tell you what your mahogany tilt-top table is worth.

You have to know how to use the directories or they can be overwhelming; there are appraisers for everything, from Impressionist masterpieces to laundry and dry-cleaning equipment. What you should look for in your region are appraisers listed under personal property, which includes antiques, fine arts, gems, and jewelry; or those in specialized areas, such as Oriental rugs, antique armor, stamps, manuscripts, musical instruments, or North American Indian artifacts, if you own those objects.

* See Appendix, page 136 for a list of appraisal organizations

No matter what you collect, be it guitars, violins, rare coins, or antique cars, you can find an appraiser with the necessary expertise. Even if a flood has recently ravaged your home, or your boiler has exploded, don't despair, there are experts in salvaged and damaged goods waiting to serve you.

If your local library does not have copies of these directories, the nearest museum or historical society should, or at the very least, will know of reputable appraisers in your community. Or you can contact the organizations directly.

Other good sources of appraisers are friends and neighbors who have had satisfactory appraisal experiences, ads in the yellow pages, or in antiques magazines and newspapers.

The specialized arts, antiques, and collectibles press is an important resource because these publications contain a wealth of information for everyone, from the beginning collector, through the passerby who just happens to own antiques and art, to the professionals who work in this field. We refer to it repeatedly throughout this book as a good place to learn more about the specific topics we discuss here.

Because there is nothing more annoying than a book that tells you how to learn more without telling you where to learn more, we are going to stick out our collective neck and list the major publications of this field in the Appendix, while apologizing in advance to newcomers we might have missed, or those who have gone out of business between the writing and publication of this book.

Appraising the Appraiser

Once you have a list of three to five appraisal firms, you should phone each and ask some initial questions. Things such as how many years they have been in business; what references can they supply from banks, lawyers, and insurance companies; where they have studied; what courses they have taken; whether they will give you names and phone numbers of some of their clients; and is it possible to see a copy of a typical appraisal that they have done?

Naturally, appraisers cannot and should not give out their clients names without first obtaining their permission; nor can they hand out copies of actual appraisal reports. Would you want anyone else to know how much your Chagall lithograph is actually worth? Of course not.

Confidentiality is an important element in this profession. However, while respecting client privacy, no respectable firm should object to your search for information about their business practices. Most actually welcome it and respect customers who investigate firms they intend to hire.

By the time you get this far you will have definite vibes about the people you are questioning. Those who get huffy you can eliminate immediately; life is too short for huffy appraisers. For the rest, the next line of inquiry should be aimed at determining the extent of the appraiser's knowledge.

Therefore, your questions should become more specific. What is their field of expertise? If it is antique furniture, is there someone in the firm whose training complements theirs? In our case, we reinforce each other: Jeri specializes in sterling silver, china, porcelain, glass, and vertu, while Helaine handles furniture and paintings. We don't appraise jewelry because it requires an appraiser with special tools and specific training; instead, we recommend colleagues with the proper expertise.

Next, you should ask what the appraiser does when she/he does not know about a given item. Responsible members of the profession will tell you how they conduct their research and what sort of network of other experts they can call upon as needed. Finally, ask what they charge. If it is not an hourly or fixed fee, watch out. Any percentage arrangement of the value of the goods is an unethical way to operate because of the obvious danger of overvaluing your goods.

Appraiser's Training

How do appraisers get their training? There is now a formal degree called Valuation Sciences, which is new to this country and available at only a handful of colleges. ASA puts out a pamphlet about these programs. But many extremely competent appraisers have picked up their knowledge in a less structured way. The professional societies conduct high quality courses and sponsor conferences and lectures, where specialists share their expertise. In fact, the annual conventions of these organizations are replete with seminars and workshops and are primarily learning experiences. They are wonderful places to get information and build networks. We each go to at least one a year, or as many as we can afford to take time away from our business to attend.

An example of this continuing education is the two-day seminar called Cornucopia IV, which ASA sponsored in cooperation with the Colonial Williamsburg Foundation in 1984. Workshops covered old silver, English ceramics, the intricacies of American and English furniture, and folk art—quilts, textiles, metalware, pottery, paintings, sculpture, weather vanes and memorial pieces. They were led by the various curators of the foundation.

Appraiser's Tools

An appraiser uses two kinds of tools—those physical utensils which can fit into a kit, and the more subtle qualities that are a combination of inherent ability and insight gained over time.

The former include a flashlight, tape measure, jeweler's loop and an ultraviolet light (sometimes called a black light); a Polaroid camera, flash bulbs, and film; yellow legal pads, a substantial supply of pens, and a stack of contracts. Because we have been known to lose these items regularly, we are now developing the F&S attachable appraiser's kit, using magnetized recall of our instruments and handy velcro straps.

Beyond these material aids, a good appraiser must have eyes that truly observe, sensibility, and experience to be able to pick up subtle clues not apparent to the untrained individual. Appraisers must be able to spot "married pieces," those period objects that have been brought together from two separate places and made to appear as one.

A good example is a pine bachelor's chest we appraised, whose top extended six inches beyond the frame. The owner had been told it was particularly valuable because it was so unusual; in reality, the top was an old one which had replaced the original at some point after it was made. It was a "married piece" because the frame and the top did not start life together.

"Assembled pieces" present a similar challenge. Recently Jeri appraised an English Victorian fish set with mother-of-pearl handles and sterling silver ferrules. She quickly saw that the handles had been replaced because they were shaped differently. This lessened the value of this flatware by more than one-third.

Caveat Emptor

With all this said, remember there are no laws yet governing the appraisal profession. The government is not looking over your appraiser's shoulder. No state supervises, tests, or regulates personal-property appraisers, and only a few require that real estate appraisers hold real estate broker-salesman licenses. BSB, buyer and seller beware, is still the defining rule in this business. There is no court of appeals to which you can go when you find you have been taken. This is why it is important to be certain that you are dealing with knowledgeable and ethical appraisers.

Testing the Appraiser

This game is not quite the same as catching the raccoons who have been overturning your trash cans. It is a much more subtle approach, which we call "client generated traps."

For example, right after we went into business together, we received a call from an attorney who engaged us to appraise five pieces of furniture belonging to one of his clients. We arrived at a stunning, spacious, contemporary house overlooking the mountains in western Virginia. There was a stream running through the property, and a glass enclosed bedroom jutting out over it, complete with an adjacent Jacuzzi. There was also enough Louis Somebody furniture to make it clear why the gatekeeper's cottage was occupied by the local chief of police.

We were met by a secretary, a bodyguard, and a housekeeper but had absolutely no idea who the owners might be. After we had appraised the five pieces, we advised the secretary that there were other, more valuable items which should be properly appraised and insured. She immediately picked up the phone and made a long-distance call to the owner, who wanted to speak to each of us.

He first asked Helaine about the two identical tables flanking the fireplace in the living room—what did she think of them? She looked at them, handed the phone to the secretary, walked around each and crawled underneath, tore her stocking, returned, took a deep breath and said, "One is authentic Louis XV; the other is a very fine 1920 reproduction."

"Mmmm," was the total response.

Then it was Jeri's turn. He wanted her opinion of two Chinese Export porcelain teapots which were sitting on a shelf in the cupboard. The first one was an eighteenth-century piece; the second, a very good Mottahedah reproduction, which could have been made yesterday.

Obviously we both passed his impromptu examination because we got a contract on the spot to appraise the entire house, including a valuable library of art and antiques reference books.

Of course, if you are expert enough to conduct a "trap test" like this one, you do not have to stay up nights worrying about hiring the wrong appraiser. Most people are not in a position to do this, but you can create your own modified version.

For example, when a perspective appraiser arrives to see the size of your job and set up an appointment for the actual appraisal, you can ask what one or two small items are worth and then check them out with another appraiser or a specialist dealer. However, if you plan to do this, you should not sign a contract until you have completed your research. Or you can use an object you own, whose value you know, to determine at the first appointment if the appraiser is genuine or just an articulate knave.

Actually, Helaine became an appraiser because of an accidental "trap test" she didn't know she was setting. She and her husband, Burt, hired an appraiser fourteen years ago to value the sterling and antique furniture they owned at that time. Among the items in their house was an eighteenth-century style dictionary stand. They had made it themselves and had lovingly stained it and whacked it with bicycle chains. Burt had even gone to the trouble of installing instant worm holes by inserting a thinly grooved nail at various angles. When this courtly gray-haired appraiser showed up and identified it as a genuine eighteenth-century piece, Helaine decided to go back to school; the rest is history.

Decisions, Decisions

Once you have found the person to do the appraisal, signed a contract, and arranged an appointment, here is what you can do to bring down the cost.

First, decide whether you want a room-by-room or a collection appraisal. The former is more logical, cheaper, and less work because each room has its own existing organization. All you need to do is go through your house and list the pieces you want appraised. A list is an essential timesaver, but if you are one of technology's children, have been raised with television, computers, and calculators, and have never held an old-fashioned yellow lead pencil or a paper pad in your hands, we give you permission to use a tape recorder.

When making a list, leave plenty of space next to each item so that the appraiser can write in proper descriptions, or be sure you have extra reels of blank tape. Finally, don't forget the things you have put in the attic, like that lovely old nest of tables you intend to refinish someday. Even in its present state, if it is old, it is valuable and should be brought out of storage for the appraisal.

If you opt for a collection appraisal and you want to save money, bring all the items in your collection to one place in your home and make a list of them. For example, say you collect chess sets. Some are displayed in a breakfront in the living room, but many more are stored. Assemble them on the dining room table so that you are not paying the appraiser to crawl around your attic.

If you don't do this, your collection appraisal bill can double or triple. We recently did a job where the owner insisted on conducting us through the house for each of his different collections. First we saw all the hooked rugs, then the sterling, then the Indian splint baskets, and so on. It was the way he wanted it, and apparently he could afford it, but it is an expensive method of doing business.

Even a room-by-room appraisal requires organization, because there are all those items in every home which are not left lying idly about. In this modern era without servants but with resourceful thieves, many people put away their silver in odd places (camp trunks, typewriter cases, the cat's traveling box) and store the fine china and crystal, which should not go into the dishwasher anyway, behind the shelf paper and light bulbs in those out of reach kitchen cabinets originally built for basketball players. You must organize all this for appraisal day. Fortunately, this hiding and subterfuge becomes unnecessary after you have had your appraisal and purchased fine arts insurance.

If the silver is hopelessly tarnished, you may want to go as far as cleaning the hallmarks, if you can find them, to make the appraiser's work quicker and easier, but wear rubber gloves and don't touch your face and eyes while working with silver polish, or you too may need cortisone ointment.

Separate the sterling and silverplate. The latter is often not valuable enough to be included in an appraisal, unless it is antique (made before 1880) or incredibly intricate. If you have a serving tray with nymphs, swans, or entwined lovers, don't put it aside. Remember, also, that there are people who collect American plate. If you own some that you want to get rid of, consult your local library, museum, or historical society for books about silverplate, or ask your appraiser how to find collectors who might be interested in buying it.

If you don't know how to tell the difference between sterling and plate, don't sulk; it is a skill not possessed by ninety-eight percent of the human race, who have nonetheless managed to live rich, full, and absorbing lives. The good news is that it is easy to distinguish between them once you have the magic clues.

Plate is usually marked as follows: EPNS (electro-plated over nickel silver), or EPC (electro-plated over copper); or it might say Sheffield, or extra quality plate, or silver soldered. Often sterling is either marked "sterling," or 925, or it is hallmarked.*

Dealing with Your Appraiser

Some important cautions. Do not expect the appraisers to put things away; that is not their job and can be done by less costly helpers, like household servants, should you still have them; children, if they are old enough not to drop and break things; or spouses, some of whom work for free. Questioning the appraisers as they traverse the house is okay and your impatient curiosity is understandable; after all, they may be about to discover an object that will allow you to retire. Remember, though, that if you hover, bother, and pester them, you are going to lengthen their stay and fatten the bill.

Finally, be sure you have given them all the information you have concerning the history of the pieces you own. This is known in the trade

---

* Hallmarks are a series of symbols denoting where the piece was made and containing the maker's personal letter or symbol.

as provenance. If your Governor Winthrop desk once graced the home of a secretary of state or a famous collector, if it has ever been exhibited, if it has been discussed or pictured in a book or auction catalogue, if it came from a well known dealer or a prestigious auction house, you should not suppress this information. You should give the appraisers copies of bills, receipts, photographs, catalogs, and books that refer to your valuable possession because all of this information affects its value.

Another way of reducing the cost of an appraisal is to keep a record of your collection as you go along. *The Kovels' Organizer for Collectors,* by Ralph and Terry Kovel, provides an easy way to keep track of purchases. Each page contains a standard form with room for a photograph and description of each object; its history, provenance, and condition; how much it cost; when it was purchased and from whom; who appraised it; the appraisal valuation; who insures it; and, for collectors who do a lot of trading, to whom it was sold, and for how much.

This kind of information, all in one spot, is extremely useful to collectors. It becomes a sort of running diary, a history of the chase. It is also invaluable if something is stolen, because it will allow you to identify it, should the police retrieve it.

We know collectors who have created their own organizers, using everything from an old-fashioned school composition notebook, the sort that children used to write in when people still used pens and pencils, to a brand new home computer that spits out data about dairy creamers and depression glass at the push of a keyboard button. ·

Inventories

Now, we wish everything you owned deserved a biennial visit from a famous appraiser, but that is rarely the case. What are you supposed to do about your garden-variety possessions? They may not warrant fine arts insurance but, if the house burns down, it will cost a great deal to replace them. How do you remember what was there after the trauma of loss, and prove to your insurance company what you actually owned? You create a written inventory.

This is something you can do yourself rather quickly, and the Commercial Union Insurance Companies* have published a useful booklet called the *Personal Household Inventory Record* to help you do it. It contains a room-by-room listing of the usual items found in the average American home. Next to each category, such as the rugs, tables, and chairs in the living room, is space for the purchase date, purchase price, and current value. The company also recommends taking photographs of every room, and close-ups of individual items.

F & S's Quick Tips

- CAVEAT EMPTOR: THERE IS NO LICENSING OF APPRAISERS
- THE PROFESSIONAL SOCIETIES DO HAVE STANDARDS
- DON'T BE AFRAID TO ASK, QUERY, PROBE, AND QUESTION
- PREPARATION FOR AN APPRAISAL WILL SAVE $$$$
- KEEP RECORDS OF YOUR COLLECTION
- INVENTORY YOUR GARDEN-VARIETY POSSESSIONS

* One Beacon Street, Boston, MA 02108

Options

If it were an absolute cinch to turn things you don't want into things that you do, money would probably never have been invented. People would have gone on bartering. It must have been the annoyance of carrying around all those cabbages, spears, beaded necklaces, and leather sandals that first tempted early man to make coins; it probably was the weight of those coins that pushed slightly later man toward paper bills.

(We thank early and slightly later man. Can you imagine the mess we'd be in today without them? Can you see us, with our digital watches, calculators, BIC pens, and pantyhose, trying to pay for a Big Mac or a ticket to the U.S. Open?)

Whatever the period in history, whatever the prevailing currency (polished stones, shekels, doubloons), one constant has always prevailed regarding commerce—the need for a meeting place where buyer and seller can hack out a deal.

Which brings us to the First Cardinal Rule of Exchange. Whatever the aethestics, value, or historical significance of an object may be, what is going on in the marketplace determines how much you can get for it. Van Gogh's Arles paintings were just as beautiful in the 1890s as they are today, but he had no customers. So, as you contemplate your original Dali drawing or early American primitive, remember that, to sell anything, all you need is a willing human person, well-equipped with some form of money, preferably lots of it, in the identical place as the article you wish to unload.

Which explains the Second Cardinal Rule of Exchange. To sell anything profitably, with minimum harassment and hassle, you must create an ideal market condition. That's why you hire professionals.

The question here is—what is your particular ideal market condition? Should you cart your stuff to the nearest auction house or thrift shop? Does it belong at a flea market or at your cousin's consignment shop? Should you arrange a house sale? That's what this section is about—your market options.

Chapter 5

House Sales

If You Sell Everything, There is Nothing Left to Fight Over

LOS ANGELES, Dec 1 (AP)—A live-in housekeeper's dream of a Christmas trip to her homeland, El Salvador, evaporated when the old raincoat in which she had kept $675 was sold for $1 at a family garage sale.

The housekeeper, Silvia Esperanza, said she had not told her employers, Marilyn and Joseph Kove, about the old pink coat, in which she had been storing money since August for the trip and for medicine for her 11-year-old son, who has hepatitis.

The Koves' children sold the coat last weekend at a garage sale for $1, Mrs. Esperanza said.

"I feel real bad that I sold the raincoat without looking in the pocket," said Danielle Kove, 11 years old. "I feel bad that she is going through all of this pain. She doesn't deserve it. She is like a second mother to me."

Mrs. Kove said she would give $50 to the buyer of the raincoat if the money was returned.

The New York Times, Dec 2, 1984

We look in pockets before we sell!!!!! As a matter of fact, we shake out cuffs, unfold linens, feel inside linings, run our well-trained fingers along hatbands, lift the tops of sugar bowls and teapots, and check the interiors of all handbags, suitcases, cat carriers, typewriter cases, chests of drawers—anything and everything that constitutes an enclosed entity—before we put it up for sale. "Empty" is another one of our mottos. We even inspect the cardboard filers that clients leave inside the metal file cabinets they want us to sell, because one of us had a mother who filed her diamond bracelet under *D* whenever it was out of the safe-deposit box. We routinely go through button boxes in search of gold and silver thimbles and once found a silver thimble worth over $50. If we ever decide to give up this business, we can certainly land jobs with the U.S. Customs Service.

Take it on faith that you will avoid a number of incredibly debilitating errors if you hire experienced professionals to run your tag sale. Unintentionally losing something of value, like Mrs. Esperanza did, is only one of them. The others, in no particular order of importance, include: over- and underpricing; the absence of ambiance; leftovers; nervous breakdowns.

Overpricing and Underpricing

The only way you can know what your possessions are worth in today's rapidly shifting market, if you don't hire experts, is to do your own research. This is quite possible if all that you want to know is the value of a pair of celadon lamps inherited from your mom. Since a lady we know named Sally lives only thirty miles north of New York City in Westchester County, she decided the easiest way to find out if her lamps were really worth as much as her mother had said would be to take them to one of the city's major auction houses for a free sales estimate.

Now, there are degrees of free. It is true that auction houses do not charge to appraise items customers bring to their front desks. But Sally had to get the lamps to the auction house before she could benefit from this service. She could hardly lug them on the train; they were too large. She had to drive her car into the city and find parking.

Sally's search for parking took an hour of her time, and cost her $21. She landed in a garage four blocks from the auction house. She had to cradle her lamps, one in each arm, and hope she wouldn't slip on a banana peel.

Even though the lamps were heavy, she made it. The young people at the desk of this particular establishment all had English accents, looked like the models on Vogue and Esquire covers, and had gone to school in London to learn how to stare through customers. It seemed to Sally that they particularly enjoyed ignoring frazzled, suburban ladies gripping large breakables wrapped in bulky bed pads.

When the ceramics appraiser finally swept in, he announced that her lamps were "copies," most probably made in Europe in the late nineteenth century, not the early genuine Chinese or Japanese ware she had believed them to be.

Sally's heart sank; she had been mentally spending the lamp proceeds as she dreamily drove into town. "Copies" meant that Mother had been wrong—they weren't worth thousands. In fact, this auction house was not even interested in selling them for her. The young appraiser did, however, admire the old glass fonts placed on the vases when they were converted to lamps.

"They don't make fonts like that anymore," he sighed, "they will definitely help . . . you might get $500 for the pair." Sally crept away, feeling like a Democrat caught trying to crash President Reagan's inaugural ball.

On the way home, there was an accident on the parkway. The car in front of Sally's stopped short. Sally stopped short. The car behind her did not stop short enough. Sally felt a sickening thud and heard an ominous shattering sound. She put her forehead on the steering wheel and refused to look.

When she opened the trunk, she saw that only one of the lamps was damaged, its glass font in smithereens. Miraculously, its base and the other lamp were intact. Sally immediately surmised that a cockeyed pair of lamps, one with font, one without, was no longer worth $500. She decided she had better love the lamps. She spent $25 to have the remaining font removed and $150 to buy new shades because the old ones were too large for lamps which had shrunk eight inches in height. The car repair came to $1,012, but fortunately Sally only had to pay the $250 deductible.

Too bad she did not know about us.

If you have the contents of a whole house to sell (which happens when parents die and the heirs do not want their possessions, or when their children start arguing about who gets what, or when you are divorcing and cannot divide your chattels without a major confrontation over every single knife and fork), remember this: If you sell everything, there is nothing left to fight over. Having a professional appraisal definitely lessens the potential for dissension.

But if you choose Sally's method, it will take the better part of a decade for you to attend the tag sales and auctions, visit the flea markets, thrift, and consignment shops, and read the hundreds of magazines, newspapers, and books that cover the "valuables" scene, to learn enough to price your possessions correctly. Underprice them and you're robbing yourself; overprice them and you'll have to hire professionals anyway to run the second tag sale you will need to dispose of the large number of items no one bought because they were too expensive.

This is no joke; it really happens. We once got a call to get rid of leftovers from a sale which was run by a competing firm. What was left was ninety percent of the original stuff. How did we know? We had estimated the job in our customary way and had lost it.

Why was so much left? It was all overpriced. The clients had been beguiled by our competition's assurances that they would make them millionaires. What they made them was exhausted owners.

There is a fine line between pricing high enough to haggle, and overpricing yourself out of the market. It's called "pricing to sell" and it is true whether you are in Mishawauka, Indiana, Boston, Massachusetts, or Eureka, California.

The Absence of Ambiance

Would you go to your favorite boutique or department store if the mannequins looked like King Kong and the clothes had been dumped on the counters?

Of course not—half the fun of shopping is the ambiance. That little black dress with the pearls and handmade silver belt, the Sherlock Holmes trench coat, and matching umbrella—these are the items that get you into Bloomingdale's, Neiman Marcus, Saks and I. Magnin.

The same is true of houses. There's a reason Beverly's mother's dining room was impressive. The Sarouk rug complemented the carved oak table; the glass crystal cabinet shimmered in the light of the brass chandelier; the samovar painting, though clearly not executed by Rembrandt or El Greco, showed to advantage over the intricately carved sideboard. Take it out of that room, and it becomes an ordinary late nineteenth-century representational painting by an unknown artist. Now, whether it is in or out of the dining room, we cannot turn it into a masterpiece worth millions. But we can get more for it in its natural habitat.

Ambiance is everything. For example, the evening before a sale, in a New York suburb, we decided that a huge baker's rack, six foot high and five foot wide, overpowered the tiny kitchen of this vintage Tudor home. It was a lovely old piece, made of iron and brass, and we knew it would look terrific if we moved it to the dining room.

After we had managed to get it stuck in the doorway which separated the dining room and kitchen, we deduced that the rack must have been built inside the house. We scratched our heads, called our husbands and kids, measured, pushed, and shoved. The combined higher education of the four adults on the moving team exceeded thirty years, but it took sixteen-year-old Debbie to figure out how the rack had been constructed in the first place.

This moving job took us four hours, three of them spent wrestling with the baker's rack, and the fourth, disconnecting its parts and reassembling them under Debbie's expert direction.

Was it worth it? Of course—we got an excellent price for it.

Leftovers

Alas, what you have to sell is rarely of uniform value. Your mother may have owned antiques, silver, handmade tapestries, and old jewelry, but she also had a barely functioning toaster, a cracked crockpot, and several side chairs with broken backs. This is nothing against your mother, who was obviously a splendid person. Everyone has household junk.

But it is the "good" items which draw in the crowds. They assure you that, if merchandise is priced correctly, just about everything will sell. This is House Sales Rule #1: in order to get rid of the leaking steam iron, you have to have some sterling and vintage clothing to attract a large audience. And House Sales Rule #2: if you hire a firm with a good reputation you are halfway there, because you tap into the clientele they have already established.

For example, there was the "puzzle house" of Providence, a beautiful fourteen-room Dutch colonial, which had been owned by the same family since 1872. And, since 1872, no member of that family, nor any of their servants, had thrown a thing away.

The house was so cluttered with objects that the first time we saw it we really thought it was listing slightly to one side. There were wonderful, unique items, and there was an ocean of junk.

The puzzle had to do with what can only be described as a vast array of unassembled articles. There was a fine group of old, toddler-size dolls, a collection so outstanding it must have been put together with great care. Why were they in pieces? Why did we find the heads in an attic camp trunk, torsos in a wicker laundry basket, assorted other parts neatly stacked inside an orange crate? Where was the top of the Renaissance Revival sideboard which stood in the dining room? Would we find it? And why was one room in the basement filled with empty bottles, carefully segregated by color the way they are at the recycling depot, and standing like toy soldiers at attention?

No Time for Questions

There was no one to ask. The owner was deceased and the heirs did not live nearby. The house had been sold and the contents had to be removed quickly. It was clear we faced a monumental task. There was no time for questions.

We started with the attic. The first indication that the world's largest supply of empty bottles was not our only problem came when we found that a window had been left open and the Providence pigeons had been here en masse. There were pigeon droppings everywhere. Helaine dashed to her car and returned wearing a black Vintage World War I gas mask. "I always carry it with me!"

Helaine's attic salvage operation solved some of the puzzles. She located the top of the sideboard in one of the maid's rooms; reassembled, the piece was a beauty and brought $3,000 at the sale. She also found an old wicker sewing box filled with letters. One of them explained the dolls. It read:

> Dearest Emily,
>
> I didn't mean for you to get so upset. Your dolls have not been kidnapped and dismembered by Capn Kidd. I did it, 'cause you hid my skates. I'll help you put them back together and will never do it again, Hah, Hah, 'til next time.
>
> Your loving brother,
> Edgar

Edgar must have been given to tormenting his sister and the collection was probably abandoned when Emily grew tired of restoring her dolls. We, however, labored like a pair of German toymakers before Christmas. We managed to get all the parts matched up in time for the sale—twenty dolls in all, which sold for between $350 and $700 each.

Exotic Finds

Edgar was not, apparently, the only melancholy member of this family. Jeri's son, Ben, found a pair of embalming gloves in the cellar. Had some ancestor been an undertaker? Not too far from the furnace, he stumbled over a vintage fuel can full of gasoline, next to a box of gun powder, and a loaded hunting rifle. These people must have liked to live life dangerously.

We also discovered a bronze box containing the ashes of some-body's grandfather, complete with a suicide note. Two customers at the sale flipped over it—an antiques dealer, and a hairdresser who specialized in the occult. In America, there is a customer for everything.

There was more, much more—vintage clothing, including six wedding gowns from 1820, 1870, 1920, 1940, and 1960; an 1880s mourning dress of black and purple silk, with a magnificently draped peplum; maternity clothes from all periods; and hats that would make even Boston ladies jealous. There was Tiffany silver; cut glass, and sterling powder jars; antique furniture from the Renaissance Revival period (1860–1890); vintage linens; silk kimonos; Life magazines going back to the forties; a collection of old Christmas ornaments that Santa would have killed for; and enough sterling silver hollowware and picture frames to empty several supermarkets of their silver polish supply.

But—there was also so much trash from this house that it filled sixty plastic lawn and leaf bags. Daily we would add to the string of fat green dwarf soldiers in front of the house. Nightly, the local trash pickers would make a mess of them. Daily, we would reassemble them, waiting for the town's bulky waste truck. They never came; who could blame them. We were clearly exceeding any reasonable trash quota.

There was only one solution. We started exporting refuse. It is not easy, believe us, but every night we would sneak a few green dwarfs into the dumps of nearby towns. Our hearts beat fast, the adrenalin was pumping, because we were sure we'd be caught. What happens to business women accused of exporting garbage without a license?

Finally, we decided to hire a private carter who promised us everything and never showed up. Desperate, the day before the sale, we spied a half empty garbage truck lumbering along a street three blocks from our Puzzle House. By this time the puzzle was—why had we ever taken this job? Jeri thought fast, swung her new Mustang in front of the truck to block its passage, while Helaine jumped out and negotiated a deal. These guys actually came, but only because it was clear we would pay anything, **ANYTHING!**

The Last Mile

The night before the sale we were still working late. The house had been transformed. It was clean. The furniture had been polished and the highlights of the wood were shining in the soft lamplight. The large pieces of silver sparkled in the dining room; the flatware shone in its fitted case. We were in the enclosed sun porch just off of the living room, arranging small silver pieces in the velvet display cases we use.

We had advertised the sale extensively and knew that soon we would hear the rumble of arriving autos bringing the all-nighters, those courageous folk who sleep in their cars to be at the head of the line. Jeri was sorting the cards with numbers on them, which we hand out in the morning on a first come, first serve basis.

Numbers are our attempt to avoid starting off with a fracas. It is all part of the pre-sale excitement as people tumble out of their cars and start speculating on what they will find inside. Of course, there is not much we can do about the brisk trade in numbers that goes on as dawn breaks over our sales. We remember one sale where a dealer friend of ours paid $100 for the number one because he had looked in the window and seen a set of mid-eighteenth-century Chippendale dining room chairs for which he knew he had a waiting customer.

When the sale was over we had used every inch of our collective retailing, merchandising, and public relations backgrounds, which, combined with the high quality merchandise, made the event an enormous success. The only leftover item was the embalming gloves.

Nervous Breakdowns

It takes time, money, and effort to move a whole houseful of furniture to an auction house, flea market, and/or thrift shop. These outlets tend to be specialized, so you may have to use more than one of them. Figuring out what should go where can be harassing, as our client, Ruth, discovered.

Ruth's mother had a lingering illness and was in a nursing home. Her four children, who had been paying the bills, were simply unable to continue. They decided to sell her home in Sagamore, New Jersey, and everything in it, to get enough cash to make sure Mother would end her days as comfortably as possible.

The house sold rapidly and the task of getting rid of its contents in a hurry fell on Ruth, the only sibling who lived nearby.

Ruth's Research

Ruth called a New York City auction house and arranged for an appraiser to come at once. He quickly identified the items his firm would sell and gave her estimates of what each item would bring.

"What do I do with the rest?" asked Ruth.

This must have been a frequent query. He handed her a list of possible outlets, two pages of single-spaced copy.

Ruth rushed to the phone and started calling. Several hours later she looked at the legal pad before her and broke into tears. The orderly columns were now surrounded by circles, arrows, boxes, and question marks. She couldn't make out what she had scribbled about the consignment shop in the next town. Were they the ones who only took furniture, or was that the thrift shop in Bayside? Was it Goodwill or the Salvation Army which still had a truck that picked up donations? What had the local auction house said about beds? And where had she put that list of all the different commission charges?

Ruth decided she was having a nervous breakdown and called her doctor. He suggested she speak to her mother's attorney, who was known as the Sage of Sagamore. Perhaps he'd have a constructive suggestion. He did—us.

"Remember, Ruth," he said, "house sales come to you."

Despite the July heat, we managed to arrange the quickest house sale in the East.

The sale was lucrative, but we were exhausted. We broke House Sales Rule #3—trust no one; stay 'til the bitter end. We left while the cleaners were still bagging refuse, because they promised to put it all out front for an early morning collection.

As we were leaving for an appointment in Manhattan at the crack of the following dawn, the phone rang. It was the Sage of Sagamore. The cleaners had deposited twenty-eight bags of trash out back. The Sagamore sanitation department would not like it. They were extremely particular about the placement of garbage. If all twenty-eight bags were not placed in front of the house, they would remain out back forever.

The new owners were coming at noon. If the trash were still there, poor Ruth, her siblings, and the lawyer, would be in violation of the "broom clean" clause in the sale contract.

To save Ruth from jail, we had to travel to Manhattan by way of Sagamore, New Jersey, not the shortest route. Clad in chic white suits, donned at dawn to impress our Manhattan client, we gingerly loaded bag after plastic bag of trash onto a hurriedly borrowed wheelbarrow, and paraded them out front.

We had saved Ruth from her nervous breakdown but were about to have ones of our own.

How to Sell Everything, So There's Nothing Left to Fight Over

Since there is no computer, robot, genie, or rubable magic lamp which can bring the ideal house sales and appraisal firm to your doorstep, you have to do your own homework. But the same principles apply as those used to find a competent appraiser. (See Chapter Four.)

Good sources of referral are lawyers, banks, and insurance companies who handle estates; ads in the Yellow Pages, local newspapers, and the specialized antiques press; referrals from satisfied friends, relatives, and neighbors; and, in some areas of the country, the trade associations of house sales and appraisal businesses which are currently being formed. Many house sales firms, ours included, are strictly word-of-mouth operations—one satisfied customer telling another.

Once you have your list in hand, you have to ask the same kinds of questions you pursued with appraisers, plus a few new ones. What is their training and expertise? What are their pricing methods? What kinds of research do they do to be certain about value? How long have they been in business? Who are their clients and can you talk to them? What is their business background? Do they have adequate insurance? Can they guarantee a crowd? Can they estimate accurately how much our sale will bring? How soon after the sale will we get the proceeds? What is their track record? What is their commission? What expenses does it cover? Can we see a copy of their contract?

Any firm that does not answer these questions to your satisfaction or is not willing to show you the contract it uses, is probably not the one you want to handle your sale.

A number of these questions are particularly important. You can have the most knowledgeable soul in the Middle Atlantic states pricing your early American furniture, but if she/he doesn't know how to run a business or understand accounting procedures, is a real dud when it comes to the IRS provisions regarding house sales, and hasn't the least idea how to advertise and draw customers, you might just as well give the stuff to the kids and let them have a good fight.

When you were researching appraisers, what you really were evaluating was their training and education. When choosing a house sales firm, business know-how is as important as expertise, efficiency, past success, and honesty. We have probably lost jobs because we told people the truth about how much money their sale would bring, while others have inflated their estimates and ended up blaming the weather, time of year, pollen count, or ocean tides for the fact that the predicted crowds and money failed to materialize.

Department of Paranoia

Our families think we have become mildly paranoiac since we started this business. Sometimes our kids shake their heads sadly and whisper, "We liked you better before."

We disagree. We weren't better before, only poorer. And we are definitely not paranoid. We are sensible and realistic businesswomen, and the following list of things to watch out for when selecting a house sales firm proves it.

1. *Lax Pricing.* Beware of people who determine value via instinct or "the seat of their pants." You are entitled to know how your firm arrives at prices. Casual pricers can be costly to your budget.

2. *Commissions.* Naturally you have to know a firm's commission; even more important is what that commission covers.

    We charge twenty percent. Our services include the preparations for, running, and the aftermath of the sale. We send out mailings to our regular customers, clean all of the silver, rehang all of the pictures, polish all of the furniture, price and tag all of the sale items, hire sales and cleaning help, write the ads, provide boxes and wrapping materials, hang posters in a two-to-five-mile radius of the house to pick up the passer-by trade, and make sure that the home is left clean and tidy before we depart.

    If there are leftovers, we arrange for their removal. We provide a written valuation of all donations for tax purposes. We also give clients a statement of gross and net proceeds, which they can hand to their accountants at tax time. We inform all neighbors of an impending sale.

3. *Unincluded Items.* The client pays for newspaper advertising but we write and place all ads. Together we set up an advertising budget. If you do not tell the firm that you hire how much you are willing to spend on advertising, they can run up a large bill, which you will have to pay.

    To stretch our client's ad dollars, we work tirelessly with newspaper ad takers to get as much information as feasible in the smallest possible space. We also pull out our secret supply of code words, which lure customers to our sales. We give our clients copies of the ads along with the bills. Since this is the only way you can know that the ads you pay for have actually appeared, you might want to ask your house sales firm to do the same. This is not paranoia; we have been charged for ads that never ran.

Clients pay for the off-duty policeman, whom we hire, and the post sale cleanup, although we make all the necessary arrangements for the pick up of trash and donations.

4. *The Elongated Possession Complex (EPC).* We work with the family as they decide what is, and what is not, to be included in the sale, and we remind clients they may not change their minds after the advertising has been placed. We find ourselves repeating "Are you sure?" so much we feel like that AT&T operator who says "The new number is . . . "

But we have become experts on the Elongated Possession Complex (EPC), an affliction common to former home owners, who drop by to tell you, "You simply can't cut down the oak tree in front or paint the shutters blue;" and to divorced spouses, who keep ordering each other around. EPC has a particularly virulent strain which afflicts people who are about to become ex-owners of personal belongings.

Actually, this book started because of a violent case of EPC.

One day we were called by a family who had abruptly sold their home of twenty-five years, a lovely eighteen-room Tudor in a plush Connecticut suburb. We mean abruptly; they had ten days to clear out. They were moving some of their furniture to their new house, some to their Virginia horse farm, some to the pads of their kids. We were given carte blanche to get rid of the rest, a melange of garden-variety department store furniture, one or two early Kittinger pieces, assorted china and glassware, clothing and linens, some bric-a-brac, lamps, and pictures.

We moved what we thought we could sell to our storage facility, and arranged to donate the rest to a worthy organization. The family, we were assured, would not be around. They would be in Virginia fiddling with their race horses, or at Saratoga, watching them win. We were told that we could treat this situation as if the owners were dead.

But dead owners don't make calls, and these two couldn't keep away from their computerized telephone, into which both our numbers had clearly been programmed. No sooner had we gotten everything out of the house then they started ringing us hourly. Which items did we think we could sell? How much would they bring? What had we given away? We wondered what was going on. Why would they care? They didn't need the money. But we continued to oblige them with factual information about tax deductions and expected proceeds.

The climax came one hot summer evening in Middletown, Connecticut, where we had been feverishly appraising for two twenty-five-hour days. We had just collapsed into cushioned chairs in the dining room of our hotel, gratefully acknowledging the instant martinis the bartender was setting down on the red paper place mats, when the manager said we had an emergency phone call. Picturing all of our collective children on stretchers and in ambulances, we banged into each other racing for the phone.

It was the female half of our favorite clients.

She was missing some belts and hats. She couldn't find them at her new house and assumed she had left them in the old house by mistake. She needed them at once, and wanted to get into our storage facility to look for them. Tonight.

Our patience was wearing thin. We said we were not returning until the next day, but that we would be glad to meet her the following afternoon.

"No," she cried raspingly into the phone, "that won't do, it must be tonight."

She said she would send a messenger for the key. We explained that we couldn't let her into our storage area without us; there was property there belonging to other clients.

Meanwhile, we were nodding at each other, having diagnosed an EPC of epidemic proportions. Perhaps we would have fought it through if these clients had given us anything of real value to sell. Since they had not, we decided to dispose of the matter as quickly as possible so that we could return to our melting martinis. Cheerfully, we promised to return everything the following evening. Back in the dining room, we grabbed one of the red paper place mats and jotted down the first notes for this book.

When we got back the next evening, we found these clients anxiously pacing up and down the driveway of our storage facility. We returned their property as quickly as we could. But we're sure this lady is still convinced we stole her belts and hats.

We fight EPC, not because we lack sympathy for the emotions involved in letting go, but because we also have a responsibility to the buying public, who tend to get crotchety when they drive fifty miles, sleep in their cars, and awake at dawn to find that the acquisition of their dreams has been summarily removed from the sale.

In fact, our contract now contains a clause which stipulates that, once something has been priced and tagged, if the family decides to remove it, they must pay twenty percent of the tagged price.

This clause was not motivated by greed or paranoia. We adopted it after a traumatic early morning scene two years ago, when we arrived at a client's house to discover all the carefully tagged sterling had vanished. This was not a pleasant moment in our lives; we had advertised the sale widely and stressed the fine quality silver. We could not help but admire the resourcefulness of the thieves, who not only got a great haul, but, by waiting until we had finished the preparations, knew precisely what each item was worth.

As we were hysterically calling the police, the family explained it had changed its mind. It took some tough negotiations to persuade them to change it back again.

5. *Go Play a Million Miles Away.* One of us had a cantankerous grandfather who could deal with grandchildren only after they were eighteen years old. Before that he would smile and say, "Go play a million miles away."

We ask our clients to do the same during the preparation period and actual sale. In fact, we advise them to be in Latvia or the Aleutians if at all possible. Even for people who cannot wait to be relieved of their belongings, the reality of a house sale usually proves stressful. There is nothing like a burly customer staring at your lovely nineteenth-century drop-leaf table and yelling at his wife, "You call that something to eat on?" to send even the most tenuous possessor into tears. That is why, when having a house sale, you should be playing a million miles away.

6. *If You've Returned from Latvia, or Refused to Go.* We tell clients foolish enough to hang around that they must not let anyone in before the starting hour. Not even two minutes early, unless they've been studying riot control and cannot resist an opportunity to practice. This is because house sales aficionados are an incredibly resourceful lot. They will pose as repairpersons of air conditioners (even in January); electric, gas, or water meter readers; Avon ladies; collectors for charity; dog walkers; exterminators; petition bearers; or soothsayers to get early access to a sale that contains something they collect or covet.

7. *Reasonable Precautions.* We make sure all outdoor walks are swept before a sale so that no one falls down and sues us. Although we carry $1,000,000 worth of insurance, which covers theft, injury, and all known disasters, including typhoons and tornadoes, we just do not like being sued. This is not paranoia, it is plain common sense.

For winter sales, if they occur in the Northern Hemisphere and there is snow on the ground, we have been known to send for a dump truck of sand or several tons of chemical ice melter. If it rains, we cover rugs and carpeting with towels or plastic to protect them. We have learned the hard way to deliver chandeliers to customers only when we can turn off the electricity before taking them down. Next to being sued, the activity we dislike the most is being electrocuted.

8. *Dealing with Thieves.* All kinds of nice people come to tag sales— dealers, collectors, newlyweds, college students, bargain hunters, neighbors who just want to see the house and the way people lived—and local thieves. The latter represent a tiny fraction of the customer population, but cause a lot of grief. If you bring up the subject of thieves, we do become our most paranoid, antisocial, suspicious, cynical, and belligerent selves. Bear with us as we explain our theft-defense-program.

When we spot a known shoplifter, we alert the policeman of the need for constant surveillance. One of the reasons known shoplifters are not popular with us is that they take our policeman away from other duties, like directing traffic, and breaking up arguments.

We design the traffic pattern at each sale to minimize the chance to steal; there are no lonely corners with small items that can be pocketed easily.

No one with a large, or even a small, shopping bag is allowed in; everything must be checked at the door, as in museums. We are also wary of people dressed in commodious raincoats, particularly on sunny days, and ask them to check both coats and umbrellas, which are also super shoplifting facilities in the right hands.

At the beginning of our business life together, we did let customers use the bathroom, until one handsome lady disappeared long enough to don two lovely vintage summer dresses under her clothing and skip out of sight. Now all we have is a staff bathroom, though occasionally we still allow small children, who do not yet look like accomplished thieves, to use it.

If adult customers must relieve themselves at a F&S sale, we suggest the bushes. It's hard in winter but . . .

We also used to put our coats down anywhere, until one of our more enterprising saleswomen sold the winter coat of another saleswoman by mistake. (Yes, they both still work for us; the owner was actually delighted to get $75 for an oldish coat "she always hated.") Now we maintain a staff closet or room, where everything is locked up.

Helaine, who serves as cashier at all of our sales, memorizes the prices of all big ticket items at every sale so that customers cannot switch tags and obtain a self-made bargain. Customers must first pay for the small items that we keep in locked cases, and present a receipt, before Jeri will haul out her key ring and open it up.

We are constantly amazed at the stealing ingenuity displayed by that very small percentage of customers who seem determined to challenge us. For example, although we have customers show their receipts when they pick up merchandise, we were once fooled by an excellent forgery that got the forger a chest of drawers for which he never bothered to pay.

We would like to have our receipts lettered by a calligrapher or printed at Tiffany's, but it's not cost effective. So now, when we sell a dresser, we urge the customer to take the drawers with her/him right away, and pick up the case later. This procedure has two benefits. The article cannot be resold by mistake—there is not much of a market for dressers with gaping spaces in front—and we are pretty sure the customer will return, since not many people need stray drawers, unless they have an inordinate number of infants or cats.

9. *Stampede Control.* In the stampede that takes place as we open a sale, some agile dealers, in possession of their own peel-off stickers which they use to mark the items they want to buy, scramble about so quickly that they lay instant claim to most of the "good stuff." They must work out at health clubs, and train with marathon runners, to prepare for our sales. We're waiting for the first one to arrive on roller skates.

Lately we've noticed that even this approach is not fast enough; dealers have started going partners with their colleagues to cover more territory in the first thirty-five seconds.

This procedure can backfire. Once, while waiting for the doors to open, two restless dealers peered through the large windows of the colonial home and spotted two pairs of tables. One was a pair of painted side tables, each on a tripod base; the other, French Louis XIV style side tables. One of the dealers wanted the painted tables, the other, the Louis XIV set. They agreed to work together.

But in their haste as they rushed in the front door, they each managed to put one sticker on each of the pairs, separating them. When they realized that they had both contracted to buy one painted and one French table, they started screaming at each other. Now, there is no question that the separated tables had little value in a market that favors pairs. We could understand and sympathize with their turmoil. But ethics required that we sell the tables as marked. We were pretty sure that they wouldn't kill each other as they negotiated a "fair" way to correct the mistake.

10. *Hustler Control.* At the end of the day the hustlers arrive. Their standard pitch is, "I'll give ya five bucks for everything that's left."

You have to be prepared for it. You are vulnerable because you are exhausted. Amateurs often agree. Professionals know they must price things high enough for haggling with hustlers.

By this time we are sure most of you who are planning to sell anything have already phoned a reputable house sales firm. If you are still debating, here are two more good reasons to hire professionals:

1. Arguments. Dealers have them. Customers have them. Professionals know how to handle them. Jeri, who runs the floor and deals with customers, has a way of defusing trouble before it starts.

2. Bad checks. People pass them. We only accept checks from individuals we know who have established credit. But at one recent sale, Jeri became suspicious when a dealer did not haggle over prices but immediately wrote out a check. She called his bank and discovered the check would bounce. We called off that deal.

However, for you diehards out there, who like more than a degree of pandemonium in your lives, The Reluctant F&S Guide to Running Your Own House Sale is below.

The Reluctant F&S Guide to Running Your Own House Sale

Step One:

Find out as much as you can about the going rates for the things you want to sell. This involves attending house sales for a few months prior to running your own. Or you can hire professional appraisers to do a resale appraisal.

Step Two:

Pick a date. Avoid the obvious bad weather months if you can. Consult the *Farmer's Almanac* if you will, but remember, it will probably rain. Do not despair if it does.

We conducted a sale in Bronxville, New York, on a Saturday in July 1984 that proved George Orwell was taking it out on us because his doomsday prophecies had not occurred on schedule. The day was characterized by a torrential downpour of the basement-flooding variety. All the parkways in the tri-state area were closed, many roads were impassable, and there were dozens of trapped cars all over Westchester County. It was clear that no one but a dolphin or a seal would venture out of doors, and they are not on our list of preferred customers. All directions in the newspaper ads were from the nonfunctioning parkway adjacent to the house. It was obviously foolish even to go.

Still, when we arrived at 6 A.M., crowds waited under multicolored umbrellas. We had to give out numbers. After the sale only the outdoor furniture was left. If only Noah read the ads, it also would have sold.

Step Three:
Find out from your town government if you need a permit to run a sale and make the necessary application.

Step Four:
Advertise at least one week before the sale. Ad writing is an art. Work on yours, tightening it before you call the newspaper or magazine, and then work with the experienced ad taker on the phone. The way the ad is written is crucial. There are certain buzzwords that beckon. Some of them are: silver, antiques, and estate, plus the name of any community which has become synonymous with affluence, like Scottsdale, Scarsdale, and Shaker Heights. (If you find more crowd-producing words, send them to us. When we revise this book, we'll add your name to the credit list.)

Once we wrote an ad for a major sale that concluded, "The volume and nature of this merchandise is so extensive that we cannot be responsible for injuries incurred while inspecting the property or on the premises." The sale was mobbed.

The point is: you have to make the stuff sound inviting, and use the good pieces you have as a draw for everything else. Remember to state in the ad that you only take cash. Checks tend to bounce higher at this sort of function than anywhere else.

Decide how much you want to spend on advertising. Our average sale merits a $200 investment. Always verify that an ad has run because there are publications which routinely fail to print ads but charge anyway. You can research the best places to advertise in your area by checking local publications to see if similar ads appear, or by calling the owners of antiques and used furniture shops and asking them where they advertise and what ads they read.

There are many good places to advertise. The local daily papers tend to be expensive but are a necessity to draw retail customers; a good size ad will cost $150 or more.

The local weeklies are the most reasonable. How well they draw depends on where you live.

Antiques weeklies charge $25 to $45 for an average size ad. The main one is *The Newtown Bee,* which is read all over the country.

If you have a month's lead time, and your merchandise is of a high enough quality that dealers and collectors would be interested, you might want to try the antiques monthlies, which are numerous and charge the same fees as the weeklies. See the Appendix for our list of the specialized art and antiques press.

Increasingly there are publications that are given away in supermarkets, or mailed to your home. They charge for advertising, but since they cost the reader nothing, they may be a good choice. These ads are inexpensive.

The antiques section of Friday's *New York Times* is a good investment if you live in the New York-New Jersey-Connecticut area. An ad here costs from $50 to $90.

Step Five:

Work up a single-sheet announcement of the sale and send it to local antiques dealers, used furniture stores, any collectors you know, and all of your friends and relatives. Make it as eye-catching as possible; this is when you call on your arty friends.

Step Six:

These are the supplies you'll need: tags (available at local stationary stores or five-and-tens); garbage bags; safety pins; scratch cover or other furniture polish; all kinds of glue; silver polish; cleaning liquids, window cleaners, handiwipes, old diapers, rags, paper towels; hammer and nails, picture wire (we rehang everything); folding tables, cloth tablecloths (dark colors); security cases with locks, lined with dark velvet for small items (like jewelry, vertu, porcelain animals, and other collectibles); newspapers, cartons and bags for wrapping; sales books, pencils, and pens; rope (to tie furniture to cars); plastic (to cover furniture on rainy days); extension cords (because, when you sell all the lamps in a room before everything else, you have to bring in light from somewhere); flash lights; an adding machine to record each transaction; and finally, a lockable, covered money box which you take with you everywhere, even to the john, and in which you put the money you have gotten from the bank before the sale so that you can make change.

> IMPORTANT NOTE: Even though you may already have some of these items in your home, if you calculate the cost of acquiring the ones you don't have, you will quickly conclude that you will spend more than the commission a professional firm will charge you.

Step Seven (for those of you who are still with us):
Decide how much to charge for each item and tag it. Good luck.

Step Eight:
If you expect any sort of a crowd, unless you have a very large circle of family and friends, hire sales help. The qualities you are looking for are honesty, pleasing personality, maturity, experience, flexibility, and a good sense of humor. People who tire easily are not good candidates, so indefatigability is another requirement. The ability to get along with all sorts of people is a must. It has taken us several decades to find a group of sales people with all of these characteristics.

For example, there is Marion, a four-foot, seven-inch blonde bundle of activity. Marion can sell the impossible—dirty upholstered pieces ("It'll clean up like new with a little elbow grease"); pictures with broken frames or cracked glass ("How much is a piece of glass?"); automobile ski racks whose keys have been lost ("What, do you think anyone actually checks the locks?").

Once she was dealing with a man who could not make up his mind about an eight-foot mahogany pedestal dining table. He left the sale. Hours later he turned up again, apparently unable to live without it. In the interim, someone had scratched its surface. Marion refused to reduce the price.

"You should have bought it this morning," she chastised him. "I told you you'd be sorry."

He bought it.

Even if they were not collectors when they started working for us, our saleswomen are now. Rita routinely comes early to check out the waste baskets because that's what she's been collecting since her first sale with us. And Linda, our secretary, helped us once when we were short-handed; now she doesn't want to answer the phone or type anymore.

Step Nine:

It is an excellent idea to collect brightly colored oak tag, indelible magic markers (it is sure to rain), and talented teenagers, and lock them in a room until they have made a dozen posters announcing the sale. Write out the copy carefully because most American high school students do not know how to spell. Post these in strategic locations between 5 and 6 A.M. on the day of the sale. This helps customers to find you and picks up passers-by. But be sure to check local ordinances carefully; some towns do not permit signs and others require permits to post them. Make sure that you take the signs down after the sale as we do; otherwise you may be charged with littering.

Step Ten:

Hire an off-duty policeman to man the outside. Make sure he wears his uniform. Customers pay no attention to plainclothesmen, unless they are armed.

Step Eleven:

Before the sale begins, take charge of the adding machine and cash box and ring up each sale, even if it makes people wait. It is the only way you can keep track of what has been sold and for how much money. Use only one door for entry and exit; otherwise, people will walk off with your things and skip the paying part.

Step Twelve:

If you wrap something and it breaks, the customer will blame you and want a refund. If he wraps it . . . ahha, so get him to wrap it.

Step Thirteen:

Remind customers that they must pick up large items on the same day. If they hire someone to do it, they pay.

Step Fourteen:

When the merchandise has been sold and the people have left; the money's been counted, profits calculated, the house cleaned, the signs taken down, the kids put to bed; the twelve arguments you had with your spouse have been smoothed over; and the neighbors have stopped complaining; sit down, put your feet up, and have a drink, if you still have the strength to lift your hand to your mouth. If not, crawl off to bed.

We know this gratuitous advice is unnecessary. We just figured it would be bad luck to end with the number thirteen.

F & S's Quick Tips

- TAG SALES COME TO YOU
- SEARCH BEFORE YOU SELL
- THINK BEFORE YOU SELL; EPC IS WAITING
- CORRECT PRICING IS THE KEY TO SUCCESS
- CORRECT PRICING DEPENDS ON KNOWLEDGE
- TAG SALES LEAD TO EXCITEMENT, ENJOYMENT, EXHAUSTION

Chapter 6

Auctions and Auction Houses

Remember the Compulsion to Own Syndrome from Chapter One?* Well, it's back. Of all human activities based on it, auction has to be the purest form.

Tom Porter, president of Garth's Auctions in Delaware, Ohio (twenty miles north of Columbus), recalls the day a substantial lady from Michigan, a collector of American furniture, arrived to inspect a lovely Philadelphia Queen Anne chair that was going up for auction the next day. She wanted to know how much we thought the chair would bring.

"I told her $5,000," says the affable Porter.

"Well," she said, "I don't think I want to spend that kind of money without consulting my husband. If I call him and ask him to come, can someone pick him up at the Columbus airport?"

"Sure," Porter replied. The next day a Garth employee was on hand to collect the husband, who had interrupted a business trip in Europe to attend to the matter of the Queen Anne chair.

In those days, Garth allowed smoking at their auctions. The chair was not among the first items sold. The couple sat side by side for several hours, she erect in a handsome suit and jewels, he in pin stripes, puffing away on one cigar after another.

When the chair finally came to the block, Garth Oberlander, the firm's founder, asked for and got a starting bid of $3,000. Every time she wanted her husband to bid, our Michigan lady would poke him in the ribs, a puff of smoke would billow out, and he'd raise the ante. He finally bought the chair for $9,000, by then barely visible inside a huge cloud of smoke. As soon as the ink on his check was dry, he rose, kissed his wife goodbye, and returned to Europe.

"It was clear," says the sentimental Porter, "that he loved her."

To You or Through You?

Another of Porter's recollections raises an important ethical question.

One day in 1979 the phone rang and a gruff voice said, "This is Jerome Fackheim and if you want to see my Queen Anne and Chippendale furniture, you'll have to pay your way out here."

"Where do you live?" asked Porter, fearing Alaska, Hawaii, or an American mission in China.

"Beverly Hills," was the reply.

Most auctioneers, invited to places like Beverly Hills, Kuwait, and Saudi Arabia, hop right on the nearest plane. Porter was no exception.

Fackheim, a screen writer, was a widower in his seventies without children. He had a fine collection of American Queen Anne and Chippendale furniture, which, Porter discovered, he was not ready to sell. He merely wanted to explore possible arrangements for the sale of his possessions after his death.

Fackheim was leaving his estate to a foundation called Actors & Others for Animals (AOA), a mink-lined animal shelter with a star-studded board. When he died, his will turned out to be ambiguous, giving the executors discretion over the disposition of the collection.

A year passed. Porter finally heard from AOA's executive director that they had decided to accept bids on the furniture. By this time, all the dealers on the West Coast and Sotheby's Los Angeles office were buzzing around the executors like bees about to take on a new queen. Porter evaluated Fackheim's possessions once more, held his breath, phoned in his bid, and prayed for two days. He won.

The executors had left it up to the executive director how to proceed. "Should I sell to you or through you?" she asked.

Porter told her she would realize more from an auction than an outright sale. He was correct. His bid had been $220,000; the collection brought $434,000 at auction in 1981.

Should an auction house ever buy merchandise outright from a client? There is disagreement among the auction brotherhood on this matter.

William Doyle, owner and chairman of William Doyle Galleries in New York City, the third largest auction house in the country, defends the practice. He routinely lets clients choose whether they want to sell their estates on consignment or directly to him. He believes it's a matter of service.

"Look," he says, the words tumbling one over the other like pebbles racing down a mountain, "when I go to people, they are often in a debt oriented situation. It is very tough and many just want to sell for cash and get it over with, they don't want to go to auction. It's a holdover from the Depression days, when people were raked over the coals. Don't forget, the modern auction business was built in my time; before that, all we had was English Snooty, you know, when they were doing you a favor just letting you in the front door."

Steve Fletcher, a vice-president of Robert W. Skinner, Inc., an auction house in Massachusetts, thinks there's an inherent conflict of interest in an auction house buying outright.

"I believe in the auction process. How can you promote it," he asks, "while at the same time saying, 'I'll buy your things'?" However, Fletcher is a Yankee trader at heart. While ninety-five percent of what is sold at Skinner's is consigned, he will bow to the will of a customer who is really determined to sell fast and move to Florida.

"I'll do everything I can to persuade them to go the auction route, but look, I'd be foolish to turn them away. It is a business. I don't think an auction house should ever make more than twenty percent on such an arrangement."

Many auction houses do not buy from clients; at Christie's and Phillips, it simply is not done, and a number of American firms have the same policy.

Sotheby's, the world's largest auction house, doesn't exactly buy from clients, but the firm, since 1983, a private corporation under the stewardship of real estate developer A. Alfred Taubman, lends money to dealers and collectors for up to a year, with their paintings serving as collateral. Whether the house actually takes possession of the art work depends on its assessment of the borrower's overall credit rating. If the debtor defaults, Sotheby's keeps the paintings, which could be construed as a circular form of buying.

Sotheby also advances money to major consignors, $12,000,000 in 1984; has extended credit to future consignors, both certain and conjectural; and has arranged financing for auction purchases.

All this mixing of art and high finance has further arched some already arched eyebrows. Certain dealers are dismayed at the idea of treating Picassos like pork bellies or Seurats like soybeans. Other optimistic onlookers predict that ordinary people will soon enter the collecting arena, able to finance their art purchases the way they do their houses and cars, through an artsy FHA (Federal Housing Administration, purveyors of home mortgages) or GMAC (the General Motors Acceptance Corporation), which has brought so many of you your Chevys, Pontiacs, and Oldsmobiles.

Why is all this important to the average consumer, who is standing at the sidelines of a millionaire's art market, hoping to pick up a print or a postcard? There are a number of reasons.

First of all, it is considered risky to ask just any auctioneer, "Shall I sell to you or through you?" Some might go no further than the "to you," grab your belongings for the first offer you accept, and resell them at a substantial profit. If you are going to sell your possessions to anyone—auctioneer, dealer, flea market, or consignment shop—you have to go back to square one and read the first chapter of this book again. That is where you learned why you have to be knowledgeable about everything you sell, how to become so, or how to hire expertise if you are too busy to acquire it yourself.

Secondly, there is the potential for increased inflation in an art auction market that has already gone bonkers, if more money is added to a pot currently overflowing with cash. According to an article which appeared in the *New York Times* on February 3, 1985, "The supply of fine quality art, everyone acknowledges, is shrinking against ever-widening demand from newly rich collectors and museums. The danger, many predict, is that Sotheby's and other lenders will be financing second-rate art with inflated values in order to feed what they see as a fast-growing market."

Thus, if you ever do get to the point where you've saved up enough money to buy a Dufy watercolor or a Vuillard lithograph, all you may be able to have by then is the artistic equivalent of a baseball farm team.

The third danger will only affect the quality of your social life, but that's also important. You may be invited to a cocktail party on the East Side of Manhattan next year, to which you have looked forward for months, because you've been longing to see the Klees, Georgia O'Keefes, and de Staels, only to discover, upon arrival, that they have all been reclaimed by the auction house and replaced with the same Van Gogh posters you've got in your living room.

Reserves and Presale Estimates

There are other issues which elicit disagreement among auctioneers. The practice of reserves is one. A reserve is the secret price, agreed to by seller and auctioneer, below which the auction house promises not to sell an item. The amount of the reserve is usually a bit less than the low side of the presale estimate.

What is a presale estimate? If you look at any auction catalogue, each item to be sold is listed by number, described in great detail, sometimes photographed, and has a financial forecast, say $400 to $800, which is the range within which the auction house believes the object will sell. Presale estimates are supposed to serve as a guide for both buyers and sellers about the general price range in which they are operating. Most consignors, not unreasonably, are curious to know whether they are likely to get $1,000 or $10,000 for their George III gaming table. Buyers want some idea of how close they might be to a cure for their current attack of the Compulsion to Own Syndrome.

Do presale estimates help them? Often the answer is no. They have too wide a range to be meaningful and are only slightly more accurate than weather forecasts.

For example, in January 1984, a pair of eighteenth-century paintings from the Italian School to be auctioned at William Doyle

Galleries carried a presale estimate of $20,000 to $30,000. They were from the estate of Rudolph von Fluegge, a well-known collector, and had once been handled by the prestigious Acquavella Galleries in New York. They sold for $46,000. Another painting at the same sale by the eighteenth-century artist Giovanni Paolo Panini, with a presale estimate of $25,000 to $35,000, again a $10,000 range, sold for $30,000.

Now, $10,000 this way or that may not be much to some people, but to the vast majority of Americans it is considered a good piece of change.

The standard auction house rebuttal to this sort of criticism is that auctions are volatile, particularly the sales of paintings and art objects from famous estates, which are widely attended by dealers and private collectors from all over the world. Anything can happen under such circumstances.

Yet the same relative range exists for less expensive objects, for example, the $500 to $1,500 price range to which most auction goers can relate. The presale estimate of a fine Victorian lamp, sold in 1984 at Richard A. Bourne & Company in Hyannis, Massachusetts, was $500 to $1,000; it brought $325. On the other hand, a rare Amberina cologne bottle of cut-glass, with the same presale estimate, sold for $2,200.

If your stockbroker functioned this way, telling you that you might make (or lose) between $10,000 and $20,000 on a given deal, he would not be your stockbroker for long. If your accountant said your tax bill would be somewhere between $18,000 and $29,000, you'd start filling out your own 1040. Both are hired for their expertise; if it is not readily apparent, you go elsewhere.

Major auction houses should be able to be more accurate. They have the expertise. Their staffs read like a *Who's Who* from Harvard, the Courtauld Institute in London, and the Institute of Fine Arts at New York University combined. They keep track of prices at their own sales, and those of competing houses, the way baseball stars count each other's home runs and politicians watch the polls in election years. Indeed, the major function of their public relations departments seems to be sending out press releases about the latest auction prices while the sale is still in progress. More and more today, auctions make the market, establishing a couple of new records every month.

If you decide to sell your possessions at auction, be wary of gradations in presale estimates that exceed $500 in the lower price ranges. Actually, we are more comfortable with a spread of $200 to $300. In the upper registers, where ranges of $10,000 or more are common, see if you can obtain a more specific prediction from the resident expert on whatever it is you are selling. If you cannot, get a second opinion from an independent authority. The money you spend on this research may save you from selling a valuable piece in the wrong way or at the wrong auction house.

If presale estimates are speculative and unrealistic, are reserves far behind? Often the answer is no. If the presale estimate is too high, pushed up there to lure consignors to the auction house, then the reserve may also be too high. When the bidding at auction does not reach the reserve, the house buys back the offering, charging the seller a fee, somewhere between two and seven percent of the reserve.

Reserves are supposed to protect sellers from letting merchandise go too cheaply. While almost all houses use them, auctioneer Richard Bourne believes they are unethical, and that they can damage an advertised article that doesn't sell, making it almost as undesirable as a bride who has been left at the altar.

"When a piece gets into a catalog, it becomes known," says Bourne. "If it fails to reach its reserve price, the piece gets a black eye or a smudge and is hurt by the auction. It becomes a diminished piece: it can take years to get rid of the blemish."

Do reserves matter to you? They certainly do. Most auction houses negotiate the amount of the reserve with the seller, but some houses set reserves at their own discretion. If you are thinking of selling through an auction house, you should find out what the reserve policy is and how much say you have in setting the amount.

As a buyer, if all you are after is a nice Sheraton dining room table, a set of fireplace tools, or a small watercolor for your bedroom, you should be aware of the fact that the auction house itself, which is supposed to provide you with a chance at a bargain, may be bidding against you.

Buyer's Premium

Richard Bourne is a bit of a gadfly: he also eschews the buyer's premium. This practice started in England and was introduced to the

American scene by Selkirk Galleries in St. Louis, Missouri. It solved the problem of steep auction house commissions, which had been as high as thirty percent, by charging buyers 10 percent of the winning bid, while dropping the size of the seller's commission.

Says Bourne bluntly, "There's no service to the buyer that warrants that charge. A realtor cannot charge both partners, so why should an auction house be able to? If you walked into your grocer's, and after tallying up the bill, he told you he was adding on a surcharge of ten percent just for the privilege of buying in his store, you'd walk right out."

Apparently groceries are in a different league than paintings, furniture, porcelain, dolls, and all the other treasures sold at auction. Most large auction houses charge a buyer's premium: ten percent is now the industry standard. Some smaller houses do also; others do not. It is important, if you are going to bid at an auction, to read the conditions of sale that are printed in the front of every catalog. That's where you find out the rules of the auction game.

The reason for the premium is clear. Buyers are plentiful; if you are one, you have our sympathy for not being a rarer species. It is the ex-buyer, now known as seller or consignor, who is the real prize, a scarce species to be as coddled in his natural habitat as any aardvark or great auk. According to all auctioneers, what they dream of at night, what they languish over, cherish, and fantasize about is the consignor with wonderful treasures to sell. While auctioneers do not routinely kill each other pursuing sellers, they will take endless risks and travel anywhere in search of "fresh goods."

Steve Fletcher used to go antique hunting with his boss, Robert Skinner, a man who loved cars and regarded every sharp curve in New England as a personal challenge. Once they were particularly pleased to have found a wonderful Rogers Group, a painted plaster casting made in the 1860s, which today is considered sculptural art of genre figures. It is not the sturdiest art form in the world; if you look too hard at a Rogers Group, it tends to flake. Moving one can be a challenge.

Says Fletcher, "We had a car full of stuff and were on our way home. Bob took this curve a little too enthusiastically, everything in back shifted, and suddenly we had a cascading Rogers Group and a wonderful collection of plaster dust. It was an expensive curve."

Another time Fletcher went to look at Chinese Export porcelain owned by "a wonderful lady in Belmont" who did not want her neighbors to know she owned anything valuable. "It was a fine collection," he remembers.

As he was leaving, his client warned Fletcher that the lady next door would accost him instantly, wanting to know what he was doing there. Thus prepared, Fletcher told the curious neighbor he was an exterminator called in to clean up a terrible infestation of ladybugs. When he reported the conversation to his client the next day, she chuckled and said, "Good, at least it wasn't cockroaches."

Choosing an Auction House, Part One

Auction houses come in all shapes and sizes and you have to consider many variables when deciding which of them to use. Much depends on what you have to sell. Of course unique and rare objects should be sold at auction. If you own a Tiffany leaded glass lamp similar to the one that set a world record of $520,000 at a Sotheby auction in Switzerland, a couple of Monets, or an extruded Galle vase, skate, run, or fly to the auction house that can command the largest attendance of collectors and dealers, get you the highest price, and give you the most advantageous terms.

On the other hand, if your parents have died and you are disposing of the entire contents of their home, which contains everything from valuable antiques and paintings, to the department store furniture they bought when they married and the antique waffle iron your mother would not part with, the most important question to ask any auction house is, "Will you take it all?" And what will you do with the things you can't sell at auction?

This is an important sociological issue because, despite the "homeless" and the shrinking government "safety net," it is almost impossible to give away certain things. A recent newspaper article reported the adventures of a New Yorker who wanted to dispose of his recently deceased uncle's wardrobe which included "an alpaca cardigan, a corduroy car coat, new trousers, and an Italian jacket with a Saks Fifth Avenue label." Four thrift shops refused, either because he had not donated there before, they were swamped, or they didn't like the green plastic bag in which the clothing was packed. The New Yorker was getting tired and cold lugging his burden through the deserted, wind swept, winter landscape of Manhattan. When he spied a derelict lying in a doorway, he offered the clothes to him and assumed his trek was over.

"No, thank you," came the polite reply. "I have more clothes than I need." He finally and furtively left them on the steps of a church on Lexington Avenue recommended by the derelict.

If you do not want to play Santa Claus to a society that is only interested in buying, not taking, it is important to find out how an auction house that you choose will handle all of your belongings.

The international houses—Sotheby's, Christie's, and Phillips—are not full service establishments; their main mission in life is to sell fine paintings, antiques, and the upper end of the collectibles market to important collectors, dealers, and museums for a lot of money. They will not dispose of your toaster. When Sotheby's promotes their Arcade Auctions as a way of selling moderately-valued works of art, they mean items which range in price from $500 to $5,000. Do not feel badly if you bring something to Sotheby's front desk for appraisal and they send you off to the Arcade. Some people get sent home.

Christie's seems to be interested in record prices. A survey of their press releases, which have been perking up our daily mail with proof that capitalism is alive-and-well in America, shows an obsession with numbers. Some recent headlines include:

DE KOONING *TWO WOMEN* SELLS AT CHRISTIE'S FOR
$198 MILLION—HIGHEST EVER FOR CONTEMPORARY ART,
RECORD FOR LIVING ARTIST

RECORD PRICE FOR BIEDERMEIER SET AT CHRISTIE'S
NOVEMBER 21

RECORD FOR AMERICAN FOLK PAINTING SET AT CHRISTIE'S

Christopher Weston, chairman of Phillips, summarized the 1984-85 auction year with this sentence, "£50,000,000 is the landmark we have reached and passed, thanks to an increasing number of clients with valuable items who have chosen Phillips."

If you are in this league, your biggest problem may be deciding which of these three houses should sell your Modigliani or George III sterling soup tureen.

However, do not discount the American houses if you have important works of art. William Doyle Galleries sold Camille Pissarro's 1893 "Rue St. Lazare" for $572,000 on September 22, 1983, more than twice what Phillips realized from each of two Pissarros it auctioned in December 1984.

Asked why his gallery did so much better than others with this great but undervalued impressionist painter, Doyle credits the size of the sale (135 paintings) and the standing-room-only crowd of bidders from all over Europe, Haiti, and Japan. But the real reason was quality. "It was a drop-dead picture," says Doyle, longing pouring out of him. "I absolutely loved it."

The Pissarro was part of the estate of Gertrude Meyer, who, with her husband, German financier Franz Meyer, managed to flee Berlin for Switzerland with all of their paintings in the late 1930s. After settling in New York, they continued to expand their exceptional collection.

Doyle had known Mrs. Meyer for years and, when she died, the family called him to take the masterpiece for safekeeping. "I wrapped it and carried it out myself so I could lock it up," he remembers. This is common practice for Doyle, who has been known to emerge from Park Avenue buildings, a sterling silver tea service clasped in his hands, like an amnesiac butler. "I've never been stopped," he laughs, "I guess most of the doormen know me."

Sensitive to criticism that they were "taking the good stuff and leaving the rest," many auction houses are now offering complete removal.

"We broom clean," says William Doyle. "We do the appraisal; ship the heirs the things they want; take the good stuff, anything worth over $500, to auction; buy the residue for the appraisal price; and either sell it in the secondhand market, or in one of our own tag sales."

Leslie Hindman Auctioneers of Chicago recently opened a house sales division and the Milwaukee Auction Galleries routinely runs in-house tag sales.

The question is: Who handles these auxiliary services? Not the people at the top, whose business is selling at auction. Much of the merchandise they take in as a service to clients is farmed right back out to the secondhand market. Those houses that run tag sales do it as a sideline. As a consumer, you have to decide whether you have enough "good stuff" that can be sold at auction to make up for what you may lose at the lower end of the scale.

Of course, you must understand that this issue represents a difficult tightrope act for us. While auction houses are not really our competition, when they enter the tag sale business, they are getting close. But don't worry, we are leaning so far over backward to be fair that we expect to function on a forty-five-degree angle for life.

Choosing an Auction House, Part Two

Location is an important consideration. While estates of great value lure auctioneers from every corner of the globe, ordinary folk should check out their local and regional auction houses. For example, Leslie Hindman started her own firm in 1982 when she learned, while working for Sotheby's Chicago office, that $1,000,000 worth of goods were leaving Chicago every month to be sold in New York.

There are auction houses with years of experience all over the country. Although they sell all types of quality merchandise, some houses have particular expertise. Richard Bourne enjoys a national reputation as a marine auctioneer; Skinner's is known as an authority on glass; John C. Edelmann Galleries is New York City's only rug auction house.*

Also important is an auction house's reputation for sales and expertise. To check this out, you should find out how long the firm has been in business; who its experts are and where they trained; how many sales are run each year; whether the sales are specialty (just paintings, or just silver) or general (a little bit of everything), or both; and how strong its financial position is. Don't be shy about asking for a bank reference. If it won't give you one, find another auction house.

* To learn more about auction houses, see *The Auction Companion* by Daniel J. and Katharine Keyes Leal.

It is not enough to ask these questions of the auction houses themselves; you should check their statements and printed material with people who have used their services; find out about the business reputations of the firm's officers; attend several auctions to see how well they are run and the number and quality of buyers they attract.

Why? Well, in June, 1984, Morton's Auction Exchange in New Orleans suddenly filed for bankruptcy, leaving 562 creditors who were owed more than $3,000,000. It was not the first reputable house to flounder. The bankruptcy of Trosby's (Palm Beach, Florida, and Atlanta, Georgia) left consignors and creditors with less than ten cents on the dollar of amounts owed to them. In Chicago, American Art Galleries Ltd. was raided by the FBI in 1981 for allegedly selling forged paintings, an event that put a noticeable damper on business. By April 1982 the firm had filed for bankruptcy, leaving 234 consignors with a collective loss that exceeded $220,000. As a result, a new Illinois law requires auction houses to deposit proceeds owed to sellers in separate trust accounts, money which cannot be used to satisfy creditors if the house goes under. You should find out if your state has similar legislation and, if not, whether any state agency routinely patrols the auction industry.

Finally, if you are consigning objects to a small auction house, hang around the day of the sale and collect your money then and there. If you can't do that, get it in writing when, where, and how you will be paid.

Commissions

Despite the uniformity of the ten percent buyer's premium, not all auction houses charge the same commissions to sellers. Sotheby's charges ten percent for lots over $3,000 and fifteen percent for those under $3,000. Skinner's and Leslie Hindman use the same percentages, but their dividing line is $500 and $1,000, respectively. At Phillips, consignors' commissions range between four and ten percent, depending on the value of the merchandise. Butterfield & Butterfield, the West Coast firm, has a complex system that should discourage the little guy. It charges ten percent for lots over $3,000; fifteen percent for lots between $1,000 and $3,000, and twenty percent between $500 and $1,000.

If you are foolish enough to show up at either its San Francisco or Los Angeles office with stuff worth less than $500, the firm takes twenty-five percent, and for those masochists who think they want to sell something worth less than $100 at auction, B&B collects thirty-five percent.

It is a good idea to find out what this commission covers. Is the cost of the appraisal refunded if you consign within a year? At most houses it is. Are moving expenses, and the cost of photographs for the auction catalog, included or extra? Usually they're extra. If the house ships articles to heirs, who pays? Generally the consignor. You should also inquire how soon after the auction you can expect your money. The average wait seems to be about six weeks.

Conditions of Sale

Auction houses print these conditions in every sale catalog and we suggest that you read them carefully. They are all mildly totalitarian, but houses do have different rules.

The basic package gives the auctioneer absolute discretion to refuse bids not commensurate with the value of the merchandise, and, despite the fact that he is the one who recognizes bidders, to decide who made the final bid if this is contested. It is a little like letting the batter, rather than the umpire, call balls and strikes.

Additionally, some houses give the auctioneer the sole right to divide lots, withdraw them from the sale, reject bids and bidders, regulate bidding, honor reserves by bidding on behalf of the consignor, and cancel the sale without giving any reason or prior notice.

If buyers wade through all that and become high bidder, they must pay the hammer price plus the ten percent buyer's premium (where it applies) in cash or by certified check either the same day or by the end of the next business day. Some houses accept personal checks, but buyers cannot remove merchandise until the check has cleared. Others will take a twenty-five percent payment as a deposit, with the rest due within five days. Removal, at the buyer's risk, must be the same or the next day, after which the auction house charges storage. If buyers do not pay for their goods promptly, or leave them at the auction house for more than a specified number of days (the range is one to seven), the house can re-auction them, but the seller is liable for any loss the house incurs, should the merchandise bring less the second time around.

Guarantees

There are two kinds of guarantees offered by auction houses. The first is financial, the reserve being the most obvious form of assurance that a particular item will not be sold for less than the agreed upon price. There is also the "world or global reserve," which is the guarantee a consignor receives on an entire collection.

The second guarantee refers to authenticity and here the situation is cloudy indeed. Sotheby's established its guarantee of authenticity in 1973, "the first major art auction house in the United States to offer this protection to purchasers." This is a five-year warranty, but each auction catalog carries "specifics" and "exceptions," which we advise you to read.

Other auction house catalogs run an extended gamut. Some sell merchandise "as is," without taking responsibility either for the authenticity of the goods or the accuracy of catalog descriptions, a sort of ultimate caveat emptor. Others guarantee authenticity, condition, and measurements of the articles described.

All houses reserve the right to correct catalog descriptions from the podium during the auction, and to refuse telephone bids for goods so revised. Reputable houses also allow buyers who question authenticity after the sale to return the merchandise and request funds, but this must be done, in writing, within a specific time period, and the burden of proof is usually on the buyer.

In practice, many auctioneers say they will stand behind the authenticity of anything they sell. Before buying at auction, you should find out what the policy of the auction house is.

Special Services

Auction houses offer the public free appraisals. These cannot be used for insurance purposes, but do give you an idea of what your valuables will bring if you decide to sell them. You can make appointments to bring portable objects to the front desk of most major firms and receive a preliminary estimate of their worth. If you cannot come in person, you can send a clear photograph. Some auction houses will visit your home without cost, but most charge an hourly or daily rate, depending on the time involved.

However, while the major houses have experts with impressive credentials, you have to get through the bureaucracy at the front desk to reach them. Sometimes these employees have peculiar ideas about service.

We know a woman who stopped at the front desk at a Manhattan auction house to find out how much an unusual three-by-five-inch Vienna Werkstatte enamel and silver box was worth. A dealer had authenticated its value and offered her $850, but she thought she might do better at auction.

The desk attendant, an immaculately groomed woman in her thirties who looked as though she had eaten lemons for breakfast, told the woman that she could not possibly take it to the head of the silver department because it was not good enough, but that she would "show it to someone." The clerk disappeared and just as rapidly returned to proclaim the box "a common piece which might fetch $200 to $300."

"Have you looked at the mark?" asked our friend, who knew better.

Lemons frowned; it was clear she had no idea where to look. Vienna Werkstatte used a distinctive mark, two Ws entwined, which they often incorporated into the design, so that it could be anywhere on the box. Our friend pointed to it and Lemons scooted backstage once more. A few minutes later she returned with a figure of $1000.

A relative of ours had a similar experience when she took a lithograph by Jean Dufy to one of the international houses and was told it was a fake. Mortified, she banished it to the third floor of her house. Some months later a young art historian with a degree from the Courtauld Institute, whose area of expertise is Impressionist art, was a house guest.

One morning he asked, "Why is that lovely Dufy turned to the wall upstairs."

"It's a fake," replied our relative.

He started to laugh. "Who would fake Jean Dufy?" He studied it for some time and declared it genuine.

Finally, there was the story in the *Maine Antiques Digest* in 1983 about a miniature blanket chest purchased at a Christie auction for $24,000 that was not authentic. Christie's returned the purchase price after the buyer was able to prove that the piece was a fake.

While such incidents may be rare, we believe that, if consigning to auction, you should get more than one opinion. You do not have to drag your things around; good photographs sent to different houses will provide you with ballpark estimates. If you have bought something at auction and you have reason to suspect it is bogus, take it back to the auction house and state your case. There may be times when you have to locate the reigning expert, which you can accomplish by consulting with museums, historical societies, or collectors. You can then go to the auction house armed with his opinion.

Special Problems

All forms of human endeavor have their problems, and the auction game is no exception. Here is a brief rundown of some of them:

1. Auction pools,* which have nothing whatever to do with water sports, are a way of holding prices down by eliminating competition. Dealers will unite and agree to let one of them bid on an item for which they might otherwise compete. They defend this practice, saying that it helps their customers by keeping prices low.

   It does not, however, help the consignor, who is trying to get top dollar for his merchandise. Auctioneers deplore pools because they decrease commissions and try to frustrate them by refusing to recognize known poolers. The problem is that unknown poolers pool, and the practice cannot easily be spotted until after an object has been sold.

---

* Sometimes called "rings"

2. Shills are not a rare species of bird or mammal, but individuals planted by auction houses to bid an item up. They are not popular with buyers.

3. Stand-ins bid for well known collectors and dealers, who do not want to appear at an auction and drive up prices. They are not popular with auctioneers and consignors.

4. Dumping is a way collectors and dealers have of upgrading their collections. For example, at the Miami Antiques Show in 1982, a dealer offered Jeri several brass and bronze figural cigar cutters. He unwittingly told her he had bought them at a Phillips auction in New York. Jeri realized at once that one of her favorite collectors was selling some of his second-rank pieces. She didn't buy them because every other collector would also have known that they were not top-drawer. Not everything sold at the major auction houses is always the best quality.

Auction House Contracts

If you are one of those elusive consignors about whom auctioneers dream, you do not have to accept a standard contract.

Contracts differ—our advice is to read and compare them. Some houses do not charge for insurance, others do. Penalties for withdrawing merchandise before it is sold vary, as do commissions and minimum charges. Doyle's doesn't charge for photographs, while color illustrations cost $500 at Phillips and $800 at Sotheby's.

Be aware of the hidden charges involved in selling at auction. For example, Christie's will charge jewelry consignors for gemological testing. If Sotheby's arranges to have furniture restored, it will add a service charge to the consignor's bill. While the reading of auction house contracts does not compare to the latest Sidney Sheldon novel, it is a necessary part of your research.

Emotion at Auctions

Auctions are exciting; they allow fantasy, dreams, and the unexpected into our lives. You may get the bargain of a lifetime, or be present when a house or world record is set. In such a highly charged atmosphere, it is easy to get carried away. You may attend an auction just to watch and learn, be bitten by the Compulsion to Own Syndrome, and find yourself emotionally and financially over your head because of a nineteenth-century Chinese panel or a New England Queen Anne slant-front desk.

While this cannot happen at major sales, where auction houses require bidders to register and receive a numbered bidding paddle, it can and does occur at garden-variety auctions. Even children are susceptible to the syndrome, which may have a genetic component.

For example, when Burt Fendelmen took his seven-year-old son, Barton, to a country auction some years back, the boy fell in love with a miniature eighteenth-century blanket chest. At the moment it came to the block, Burt was deep in conversation with another collector of country furniture over whether the lift-top pine blanket chest would bring anywhere near the estimate of $1,500. He felt the boy tugging at his trousers and heard a subliminal "Daddy, Daddy," but he was truly absorbed. When he finally turned toward his son, it was just in time to see Barton make the winning bid of $150. Half of him thought, chip off the old block. The other half remembered that he didn't have that much cash with him.

To help you have fun as you explore the auction game, we have developed the following *Auction Rules of Restraint:*

1. Before attending an auction, look at the balance in your checking account. This sometimes has a sobering effect.

2. If you do intend to buy, make sure you visit the showroom during the exhibition period that precedes every auction, examine the objects which interest you, ask questions about them of the auction house staff, and compare the presale estimate with what you think the piece is worth and intend to spend. If you are a regular auction goer, compare the estimate to the prices brought by similar objects at recent auctions. There is always hope that all this research will calm you.

3. If, after all, you do plan to buy one or more specific objects, decide beforehand the absolute top you will pay for each. Write this

figure in blood on your left hand and make believe you are a young girl who has just received an engagement ring: hold your hand in front of you constantly during the bidding. You do not have to use your own blood, you can use someone else's.

F & S's Quick Tips

- **REMEMBER CAVEAT EMPTOR**
- **BEWARE OF COMPULSION TO OWN SYNDROME**
- **READ THE FINE PRINT**

Chapter 7

Flea Markets; Antiques Marts, Fairs, and Shows; Thrift Shops and Everywhere Else You Can Have Fun Buying and Selling

Flea markets started in Paris, where they were called *marche aux puces* because the French thought that the large quantity of secondhand merchandise found at these open-air festivals attracted fleas. The title stuck despite the fact that this assertion has never been subjected to rigorous scientific analysis or proved one way or the other. The markets (not the fleas) quickly spread all over western Europe and Great Britain and, in the last decade, have become enormously popular in the United States.

One reason is that they are fun. Another is that you can find terrific bargains at some of them. Most flea market merchants do not have large inventories or overhead expenses and they can afford to sell for less. Finally, anyone can play this game. You don't have to go to school, win a degree, obtain a license, take a test. All you need is the merchant's instinct, a great deal of energy, something to sell, a small quantity of cash to pay for the rental of a booth or table, and you are in the flea market business.

Some flea markets are huge and sell an enormous variety of merchandise, some of it masquerading as antique. We have a friend who still remembers being overwhelmed by her first visit to Portobello Road

119

in London, perhaps the granddaddy of flea markets the world over. There she fell in love with a small, somewhat blackened knight in armor, about three feet tall from his toes to the top of his lance, whose purpose in life was to hold fireplace tools.

Our friend, who had never seen so clever an object before, believed the dealer who told her this was a "unique piece, Mum, from the 1860s it was," as well as his assurances that any silversmith or metal shop in the States could refinish her knight for just "a wee bit. The thing is, Mum, not ta 'esitate an lose 'im."

Our friend quickly named him Albert, lugged him back to the Savoy by bus, tube, and taxi, and sailed past the doorman with head held high, despite her aching arms and the stains Albert had inflicted on her smart beige suit. When her husband returned from his medical conference, he found her bathing with Albert in the Savoy's seven-foot tub.

"How do you intend to get him home?" he asked.

"Don't worry," she replied gaily, "he'll fit under the seat."

The next day her enthusiasm dragged them both back to Porto-bello Road. She absolutely had to show her husband the authentic hunt table that would be perfect in front of the bay window of the Tudor house they had just purchased in a suburban enclave near Manhattan. As they hopped off the bus, she turned very pale. Just down the road was a shop with several thousand Alberts, all newly minted and shiny, and a big sign in the window, "We Ship Anywhere."

Authenticity is a problem in all phases of the art and antiques world. The forging of paintings has reached such perfection that museum curators have been fooled. A celebrated example was discovered in 1975 at the Cleveland Museum of Art. A painting that was supposed to be by the sixteenth-century artist Mattias Grünewald, considered the greatest German painter after Albrecht Dürer, was actually the work of a German art student and restorer who was alive and well in Munich.

Does a forged painting have to take itself off to a nearly-new arts shop when the jig is up? Not at all. In this case, the dealer who sold the painting absorbed the loss, while the museum kept it for study purposes. What better place for young curators to learn about forgeries than standing in front of a classic one?

Similarly, instant antiques are not unknown. The classic case is that of the "Great Brewster Chair" at the Henry Ford Museum in

Dearborn, Michigan. The original Brewster chair was built in the 1620s for William Brewster, elder of the Pilgrim Church, as a symbol of his authority. This and a second one, constructed in the late 1600s, are the only two known to have survived. One is at the Metropolitan Museum in New York, the other in Plymouth, Massachusetts. But rumors of a possible third one had floated around the antiques community for years.

A talented wood sculptor named Armand LaMontagne, who wanted to see if he could fool uppity museum curators and dealers, took advantage of the rumor and built a third "Great Brewster" in 1969. He planted it in a Maine house and waited for it to be discovered. It was such a brilliant piece of work that a number of experienced dealers were sure it was authentic, including the one who eventually sold it to the Ford Museum. There it was proudly displayed for four years, with its own personal bodyguard in constant attendance. After LaMontagne admitted the hoax and his reasons for it in 1977, the chair was put into storage.

Elliot Sherman, a collector and dealer in Massachusetts, says he witnessed this same phenomenon when he was young, innocent, and new to the field.

"I was befriended by this outrageous character, a creative genius and raconteur extraordinaire, a college-trained chemist and metallurgist, who could create antique finishes which exactly matched the old finishes and paints; you could not tell the difference. One day, I arrived at his house to find him frantically painting this most wonderful old settle green. It was at the height of the early American painted furniture craze.

"He owned a large convertible, which stood in his driveway with the top down. As soon as he was through, he put me and another friend in the back seat and commanded us to hold the settle against the wind, while he drove at seventy miles per hour through the countryside, so that the paint would be dry when he delivered it to a very prestigious dealer. I nearly flipped when I found out who it was. We got to his shop and put the settle in the driveway. The dealer came out, walked around it, went wild over the form and old paint, and bought it instantly, despite its $1,200 price tag."

You will not find a fake Brewster chair or a wonderfully restored country settle at most flea markets, where the quality of merchandise varies. Some feature inexpensive furniture and reconditioned appliances from the forties, but at others you can buy Bokhara rugs, Victorian crystal jewelry, hallmarked silver, opaline glass, Ecuadorean ponchos, Fiesta Ware, and designer jeans.

Flea markets represent a last great American frontier of commerce; only here can a merchant arrive at the spur of the moment to sell in an atmosphere that is clearly "every man for himself." While the larger markets require advance booking of booths and stalls, many are totally impromptu.

Dealers arrive at the big markets days before the opening to set up their stalls. At smaller, one-day affairs, they come the night before and camp out. They start trading by flashlight around 4 A.M., with the real frenzy reaching a crescendo between 7 and 8 A.M.

We're not kidding about this trading madness. We remember a dealer who broke her leg in the murky dawn light, tripping over a boulder as she raced across a field to look at art pottery. While she was waiting for the medics, we saw a colleague, who dealt in steamship souvenirs, lean over her groaning body and ask, "Do you have anything for me?"

Then there was the Great Glass and China Debacle at the Topsfield Flea Market in Massachusetts. Colleagues of ours arrived the night before the market opened. Their van was packed to the roof with furniture, cartons of dishes and glassware, two cranky children, two dogs, and four sleeping bags.

They joined the long line of cars waiting to enter the parking lot the next morning. Since there was no room to sleep in the van, they decided to spend the night under the stars. But as soon as they were settled, it started to rain. And, it was not a little light passing summer shower. Within five minutes it was clear that no one could camp outdoors.

The parents grabbed the cartons full of breakables and stored them under the van. This made enough room in back for four midgets, if they all promised not to turn over or breathe. Exhaustion is wonderful, however; despite the cramped quarters, they all slept so soundly that the next thing they knew it was 7 A.M. The long line of cars was moving, and everyone behind them was honking like tugboats welcoming an ocean liner. The father jumped behind the wheel and started up, forgetting the cartons under the van. They sold furniture that day.

"In the early seventies everyone took their kids and animals along," remembers Helaine. "In fact, my introduction to flea markets was as a very young mother. Barton was two months old and the baby sitter disappointed us. So I put him in a wicker basket and exhibited him."

Flea marketeering is not exclusively for the baby-carriage set. We know a couple in their early seventies who found the flea market business therapeutic. The husband had been left listless and depressed after a long illness. His wife, who sold lace and linens at a flea market near their New York City apartment, saw that something was needed to get him back into this world. She convinced him to come along on her "picking" expeditions.

"It turned him around," she says with delight, "from feeling he was finished, it has become a full time thing which we both love. We're out every day hunting for things all over the East; not just linens anymore, we sell all kinds of collectibles—picture frames, majolica plates, penknives—whatever strikes our fancy. We have lunch and dinner out, go to auctions and tag sales, and have a wonderful time all week. On Saturdays, we sell."

This energetic grandmother bubbles with enthusiasm for her current career. "What's fun is the chase, putting yourself on the line, selecting, buying, pricing, selling, and having your taste and judgment confirmed when customers buy with relish."

In addition to all night waits, sleeping outdoors, restless children, lost animals, and the opportunity to go balmy in an electric atmosphere, flea market dealers have to grapple with the weather. The market in Chatham, New York, takes place during the first week of August and is known for its unbearable heat and rain. Once there was such a deluge that the Fendelman van found itself in a bonafide quagmire, with mud up to the hubcaps. It eventually had to be pulled out by a tow truck. But the flea market customers turned out to be just as hardy as the dealers. "It's the only time we have ever sold out, I mean every last railroad spike. Of course, we also sold wonderful country furniture that day."

The markets held at Brimfield, Massachusetts, three times a year, are the largest in the country, with over seven hundred exhibitors. They occur in May, July, and September, but it is the summer one that represents the purest form of fighting the elements. Once Jeri remembers seeking cover indoors during a cloud burst. "It was so hot I finally knew what Hansel and Gretel felt like when the old witch tossed them into the oven."

But perhaps the largest, best, and most memorable flea market of them all was the one held in the early seventies called "Portobello, New York." Fifty-third street was closed to traffic from the East to the Hudson Rivers. Hundreds of exhibitors sold antiques, ephemera, vintage clothing, rare Chinese porcelain, furniture, rugs, silver, books, quilts, weather vanes, jewelry, toys, posters, sweat shirts, sepia photographs, Art Deco lighting fixtures, and just about everything else which these ingenious and visionary traders could think of to bring.

Every known variety of ethnic food was available. There were street bands, strolling lute players, mummers, violinists, portraitists and dancers. The market was scheduled from nine to five but we felt lucky to be out by midnight.

Antiques Marts, Fairs, & Shows

There are thousands of antique shows, sometimes called fairs or bazaars, all over the country in the course of a year. The best way to find out where and when they occur in your region is to consult the specialty antiques press listed in the Appendix.

Antique shows have better quality merchandise than flea markets. Some promoters allow only recognized dealers to exhibit; others will take anyone who can pay the tab, which varies from $200 to $2,000, depending on the size, duration, and prestige of the show.

By recognized dealer we mean someone with a lot of hands-on experience, training in the arts, staying power and a reputation for reliability. Bill Ketchum, a well-known arts and antiques writer, estimates that there are only a couple of hundred dealers left in this category. Turnover is huge; he says that seventy-five percent of dealers leave the business every five years.

Ketchum is one of the defectors. A couple of badly-organized shows convinced him to look for a different career. The one that finished him off took place at an old hotel, described by the show's promoter as a "little replica" of the Taj Mahal, which turned out to be an abandoned building with stained walls and bone-chilling dampness. "It didn't much matter," says the philosophical Ketchum, "because the location was so obscure the public couldn't find it."

Is it dangerous to buy at an antiques show if the dealer is likely to turn into a vacuum cleaner salesman or butcher before you have unloaded your station wagon? It depends on the show. Some promoters and dealers guarantee the things they sell at these shows. There are professional organizations of antiques dealers listed in the Appendix, where you can get information about reputable dealers and shows.

Antique shows are good places to study the antiques scene and have fun. You can see a wide variety of merchandise, talk to and learn from many experienced dealers, get some idea about prices, find out what books to read, eat a lot of hot dogs or, at some, gourmet salads, and learn about haggling.

Haggling is an art form—some shoppers are addicted to it, while it makes others uncomfortable. The breakdown is largely geographic. Many Europeans, South Americans, and Orientals are so devoted to elaborate haggling that they feel cheated when it does not occur. Americans, conditioned by department stores and supermarkets with fixed prices, tend to be embarrassed by it.

Not all Americans. A collector of weather vanes who is also an accomplished haggler once passed a booth at an antiques show in Boston and saw a magnificent specimen marked $150. There is no such thing as an authentic American weather vane at this price. He knew he should grab it and run but he could not resist haggling. The dealer frowned when the man offered him $100, looked at the sign, turned pale, and added the missing zero.

The other advantage of these shows is that you can build wonderful family vacations around them. In the summer of 1973, Jeri and Ed Schwartz packed up their three children, then four through twelve years old, two dogs, and a tiger cat who had never been caged, but without whom eight-year-old Rachel refused to travel, and put them all in the back of the family station wagon. They were driving from their home in Carmel, New York, to a show in Ocean City, Maryland. The plan was to kennel the animals there so that the children could visit them during the week of their stay. There was a mattress in the back of the station wagon so that the youngsters could sleep while their parents took turns driving all night.

"We got as far as Armonk, about twenty miles from home," Jeri remembers, "when the cat threw up and the dog urinated. We had to remove everything and scour the back of the car from one end to the other. Rachel, now twenty, still remembers what that car smelled like."

When they got to the show, they discovered that there was no safe for Jeri's Russian enamels, which were then extremely valuable; a small spoon at that time brought $300 to $400.

"We couldn't all go to the beach together," says Jeri. "Someone had to baby-sit the enamels."

Fendelman and Schwartz didn't even know each other then, but they were already engaging in parallel activities. One March, the Fendelmans decided to combine the Ann Arbor, Michigan, Antiques Show with a family vacation. No sane person picks Michigan for a March vacation, but these two took the children, then seven and ten, out of school and, with their two Yorkshire terriers, Holly and Gwendelman, set off in their van, pulling a trailer loaded with furniture they intended to sell.

Now, you cannot take children out of school in America without making the cause of their absence an educational experience which will far surpass anything that happens in the classroom during their absence. Helaine and Burt decided to show the children Canada. Admittedly only a small portion of Canada, but it was the first trip abroad for their sons, Jonathon and Barton.

The plan was to visit Niagara Falls, cross into Canada so that they could all view the Falls from both sides, trundle along the north shore of Lake Erie, and reenter the U.S.A. at Windsor, Ontario, a stone's throw from Detroit, the entire distance being something under 250 statute miles.

But crossing any border, even a friendly one, with goods can be a hassle. You must declare all valuables by filling out five copies of a government form, and then do it again upon your return, deleting what you have sold, and presenting complete documentation of all your commercial transactions.

How would they prove they had sold nothing? Would they end up in detention and miss the show? They elected not to risk it, and told the customs officials, when asked, "We're moving."

Returning seven hours later, they were faced with a different border crossing, but the same problem. This time they decided, at the risk of hurting the feelings of the Windsor officials, to admit that, although they had tried Canada, they hadn't liked living there.

"We were a little nervous, worried that maybe they'd check," says Helaine, hoping there is a statute of limitations on border crossing violations, "and we wanted to be as friendly and folksy and not particularly obvious as possible. So what does Jonathon do? He lets go of Holly who jumps out the window and tries to bite the customs man."

Antiques Marts

A new format for the old-fashioned flea market is the modern antiques mart, which started in England and is still prominent there. It brings many dealers together under one roof, usually in a warehouse or loft, on a more or less permanent basis, with a manager in charge. The idea spread to the States, first to California, and received a big impetus in the early seventies when gas lines made people think twice about "going antiquing." They were an economical way for dealers and customers to congregate without wasting gas, and seemed about to become the "7-11s" of the antique world as they started appearing in New York, Texas, Vermont, and Indiana.

Now they seem to be withering. Some have closed in California due to increased unemployment in the high-tech field and the same is true in Texas, where the oil glut has caused an economic downturn. Their future seems uncertain.

Thrift and Consignment Shops

Consignment shops are for-profit enterprises where you can leave articles to be sold and receive about seventy percent of the purchase price.

Why do people consign? Well, say you have always hated those silver sconces that meant so much to your mother. There is nothing else you want to get rid of, and no one in the family has the slightest interest in them. You do not wish to be bothered with a tag sale or auction. A consignment shop is for you. Then there are people who like to use consignment shops because they do not want the neighbors to know they are selling their possessions.

In dealing with a consignment shop, you should be certain that you receive a written contract that specifies the amount of the commission; lists the articles you have left; the length of time you have contracted to leave them; and what happens if they are broken, stolen, torn, or nicked. Most consignment shops take no responsibility for loss or damage, and some have been known to hide consignors' merchandise, claiming that it has been stolen, so that they can keep the sale proceeds. Deal only with shops that carry insurance, have been in business for some time, and agree to be liable in case of loss. Otherwise, keep the sconces.

While thrift shops are usually thought of as benefitting charitable organizations, the majority of them actually are for-profit. Sometimes you are better-off financially if you donate what you want to get rid of to a non-profit thrift shop, if you can find one that will accept your gift, and get a tax deduction. Check with your accountant, who can advise you about the tax benefits of donations.

Thrift shops that are for-profit sell used merchandise just the way flea markets do, but in a permanent location. And, like flea markets, what you find in them is a mixed bag of junk and treasure.

Jeri has few obsessions, but one of them is thrift and consignment shops. She's a hopeless addict; the dustier they are the better. She loves to browse in them, crawl under tables and go through boxes of odds and ends. If she hears of a shop that might have something she covets, no matter where it is, there is no stopping her.

Last year while in London, Jeri heard about a small silver snuff box in the shape of a dog's head that was supposed to be in a consignment shop in the tiny town of Reigate, a small village about an hour's train ride from London.

A friend who lives in Surrey told her not to waste her time; there was nothing in Reigate. Jeri paid no heed; the very same day she was on the train.

Arriving in Reigate, her heart sank. There was the station, a pub, and a small dingy shop that appeared to be closed. Nothing else. Jeri consulted her timetable and saw the first train back to London did not pass through for two hours.

Jeri doesn't drink. She surveyed the shop—the windows were so cloudy it was impossible to guess what might be inside. She walked over and found that it was open. And inside there was a snuff box shaped like a dog's head for $75.

What does a teetotalling American dealer do in Reigate during the two hour wait for the next train back to London? She becomes an unbiased observer of English pub life. Was it worth it? You bet. She sold the box for over $200.

Helaine and Burt never paid much attention to consignment shops until the 1973 gas crisis put an end to wandering by car in search of treasure. They started exploring the consignment and thrift shops in New York City and learned how objects sometimes have a strange and circular life.

At the time, Helaine was hunting for examples of Tramp Art, which she was then researching for a book.* One day, she heard about an unusual piece that was supposed to be in a consignment shop somewhere on the upper East Side of Manhattan. She and Burt scoured the area, going from consignment shop to consignment shop, asking if anyone knew anything about a Tramp Art miniature pool table that might or might not exist. Just as they were about to give up, they wandered into one last shop on 72nd Street and there it was. They hand carried this heavy, three-foot-long piece, made of cigar boxes and crates and definitely not designed for urban bus and train travel, from the shop to the bus stop to Grand Central Station.

Their train was crowded because everyone else was leaving their cars at home, but the table provided two custom-made seats. Arriving in Scarsdale, they lugged it the last two miles to their house. But clearly a treasure had been added to Helaine's collection.

In 1975 the book was published, immortalizing the pool table. In 1982 Burt was on one of his peddling missions in Manhattan, where he had taken the pool table to show it to a potential buyer. As luck would have it, while he stopped for a cup of coffee, the table was stolen out of the locked van.

* Tramp Art is a little known form of folk art which flourished around the turn of the 20th Century. See *Tramp Art* by Helaine Fendelman, Dutton, 1975.

He reported the theft but the police did not drop their murder, arson, theft, and bribery cases to look for the table. It was never recovered. Fortunately, it was fully insured under their fine arts policy.

But six months later, Helaine received an unexpected phone call from a dealer in Connecticut. "Hey," he said, "have I got a Tramp Art piece you're going to flip over! It's a miniature pool table."

F & S's Quick Tips

- SHOWS, SHOPS, FAIRS, MARKETS AND MARTS PROVIDE:
- ELECTRICITY
- IMPULSE BUYING
- LUNACY
- HAGGLING
- A CHANCE TO SPEND AND
- WONDERFUL THINGS TO BUY

F&S's Quickest Tips

Addiction Can Be Fun

Collectors are very pleasant addicts; they may think they can walk away from something they covet, but they cannot.

For example, Sam Pennington, editor of the *Maine Antique Digest* and a long time collector of Americana, tells this story about himself:

One of his regular stops on the auction circuit is Foster's in Newcastle, Maine. At a recent sale, Sam saw an Empire mirror with a reverse glass painting of a woman seated upon an Empire sofa. It was by James Todd, the well known nineteenth-century furniture maker from Portland, Maine, and happened to be the only antique in the sale. There was a piece missing from the lower part of the frame. Pennington decided it was too rough an object and not suitable for his collection of Empire furniture. He left the auction early. Afterwards, he learned that the mirror had sold for $225.

A month later, at Julia's Auction Gallery in Fairfield, Maine, what turned up on the block? A James Todd Empire mirror with a reverse glass painting of a woman seated upon an Empire sofa. And who bought it? Sam Pennington, for $300. Says Pennington, "Collectors are finicky, just like salmon. Sometimes they bite, and sometimes they don't."

The Custodian Principle

Even people who acquire things through inheritance and think they are not collectors often find that, once they know the history and value of the pieces they have been left, they want to become caretakers for their children or for future generations.

For example, auctioneer Steve Fletcher remembers a wise old client in his nineties who had wonderful country furniture, which had been well cared for and was in mint condition. When Fletcher admired the collection, the old gentleman smiled and said, "I don't own these things."

Fletcher began to wonder, was he the butler, an impostor, or a practical joker?

"We're just custodians," the client went on, "my time for taking care of these things is coming to an end, and I'm passing the responsibility on to someone else."

Dealing with the Compulsion to Own Syndrome

The compulsion is so strong that it can cause management problems. For example, Irene Stella, a promoter of major antiques shows in the Northeast, like most promoters, runs a very tight ship. No customer, no matter who he is, can enter a show before starting time— ever. Like a racehorse who jumps the gun at the gate, precocious buyers are returned to the entrance to wait with everyone else for the starting gun.

One morning, Irene saw that a veteran dealer she has known for years was helping a new dealer set up his booth. He waved her over and, as she approached, she saw a third man inspecting the merchandise. The veteran, smiling proudly, introduced her to "my pal, Bruce." Irene promptly threw Bruce out, in spite of the fact that his last name was Springsteen.

Irene is not impressed by celebrity collectors if they try to arrive before the show opens. Confucius, Buddha, Jesus, Moses, Mohammed, Socrates, or Plato—none of them could have gotten in early either.

Pricing Problems

Buyers and Sellers are never satisfied. Try to remember these homilies when attacked by pangs of remorse.

If you think you have overpaid for something—you really haven't, you just bought it too soon.

If something sells too quickly, you may automatically assume that you priced it too low and may want it back at once. It happens to everyone.

Fashions are not just for Clothes

Fashions in antiques and collectibles are similar to ladies' hemlines; they go up and down.

If you are going to sell, it is wise to wait until your possessions are up. If you are buying, delay until the objects of your desire are down.

If you can figure out how to do this all the time, you should start writing the sequel to this book at once.

Resemblances

Beware of the Exactly Like it Syndrome, to which all collectors, acquirers, and ordinary people are susceptible.

For example, we once were called by a lady in Hartford to appraise eight bowback Windsor side chairs. She had seen chairs "exactly like" hers priced at $350 each at an antiques show in White Plains, New York.

We had been at the same show and had seen the chairs which stimulated her interest. They were beauties—they had an exaggerated bow, shaped saddle seats, nine spindles instead of the customary seven, and legs that were well turned, with an unusually extended splay. There were still traces of the original green paint on them.

So we raced up to Hartford, trying to control our excitement. It was short lived. These chairs had ordinary bowbacks, plebeian plank seats, seven spindles, bamboo turned legs, no paint, and were worth between $75 and $125 each. They were not "exactly like" the chairs in the show; they weren't even close.

Eavesdropping

Overheard by jewelry specialists Sid and Joan Cohen: "It must have been gold, they were very rich people." Beware of appearances, assumptions, and suppositions. Rely on fact.

Look Inside and Out

When buying at auction, examine things closely. An irate bidder, who had paid $82,000 for a tall case (Grandfather's) clock at a Sotheby auction, returned it because, when he got it home, the weights and pendulums were missing!

Real Treasure

It is possible to find something of exceptional value in out of the way places. It is extremely rare. But we'll tell you this lovely story to keep your hopes up.

A gentleman from Long Island bought a porcelain sweetmeat dish, circa 1772, made by Bonnin and Morris of Philadelphia, for $2 at a garage sale five years ago. He knew something about porcelain, was pretty sure it was valuable, and took it to Sotheby's for a presale estimate. You can imagine his state of pure joy as they told him it would bring between $20,000 and $30,000. When it came up for auction, the dish sold for $60,000, plus the ten percent buyer's fee, a record price for this type of object.

Our Final Word

Now that you know it all—what to collect, how to collect, where to collect, how to look at objects, hire appraisers, do research, learn, buy and sell—remember the most important thing in the art, antiques, and collectibles universe is to have fun!

Appendix

The Arts, Antiques and Collectibles Press

American Collector, PO Drawer C, Kermit, TX 79745

American Collectors Journal, PO Box 1431, Porterville, CA 93257

Antique & Auction News, Box B, Marietta, PA 17547

Antique Market Tabloid, 10305 Calumet Drive, Silver Spring, MD 20901

Antique Market Report, PO Box 12830, Witchita, KA 67277

Antique Monthly, Drawer 2, Tuscaloosa, AL 35402

Antique Review, PO Box 538, Worthington, OH 43085

Antique Trader Weekly, PO Box 1050, Dubuque, IA 52001

Antiques & Art, 2227 Granville Street, Vancouver, B.C. V6H3G1

Antiques & Collectibles, 25 Glen Head Road, Glen Head, NY 11545

Antiques Gazette, 929 Davidson Drive, Nashville, TN 37205

Antiques West, PO Box 2828, San Anselmo, CA 94960

Antiques of the Great Northeast, Bridge Street, Hunter, NY 12442

Antiquing, 301 Sovereign Court, Suite 203D, Manchester, MO 63011

Art & Antiques, 89 Fifth Avenue, New York, NY 10003

Art & Auction Magazine, 250 West 57th Street, New York, NY 10019

Arts & Antiques Antiquarian, Box 798, Huntington, NY 11743

Cape Cod Antiques & Arts, PO Box 400, Yarmouth Port, MA 02675

Cape Cod Antiques Monthly, PO Box 340, East Sandwich, MA 02537

Collector's Journal, Box 601, Vinton, IA 52349

Collector's Showcase, PO Box 27948, San Diego, CA 92128
Collectors News, Box 156, Grundy Center, IA 50638
Eastern Antiques Reporter, PO Box 948, Essex, MA 01929
HOBBIES, 10006 S. Michigan Avenue, Chicago, IL 60605
Maine Antiques Digest, Box 358, Waldoboro, ME 04572
Mass Bay Antiques, 2 Washington Street, Ipswich, MA 01938
New England Country Antiques, 4 Church Street, Ware, MA 01082
New Hampshire-Vermont Antiques Gazette, PO Box 40, Exeter, NH
    03833
New York Antiques Almanac, Box 335, Lawrence, NY 11559
Renninger's Antique Guide, PO Box 49, Lafayette Hill, PA 19444
Silver Magazine, PO Box 1243, Whittier, CA 90609
Southern Antiques, PO Box 1550, Lake City, FL 32055
Southwest Antiques News, PO Box 66402, Houston, TX 77006
The Antique Dealer, Box 2147-1115 Clifton, Clifton, NJ 07015
The Buckeye Marketeer, 16 E. Henderson Road, Suite 204, Columbus,
    OH
The Jersey Devil, PO Box 202, Lambertville, NJ 08530
The Magazine Antiques, 551 Fifth Avenue, New York, NY 10017
The National Antique Journal, PO Box 78, Charleston, TN 37310
The New York-Pennsylvania Collector, Fishers, NY 14453
The Newtown Bee, Newtown, CT 06470
Tri-State Trader, Box 90-27 No. Jefferson, Knightstown, IN 46148
Yesteryear, Box 2M, Princeton, WI 54968

National Appraisal Organizations

American Society of Appraisers (ASA), Dulles International Airport,
P.O. Box 17265, Washington, DC 20041 (703) 620-3833

Antique Appraisal Association of America, 11361 Garden Grove
Boulevard, Garden Grove, CA 92643 (714) 530-7090

Appraisers Association of America, 60 E. 42nd Street, New York, NY
10017 (212) 867-9775

International Society of Appraisers, PO Box 726, Hoffman Estates, IL
60195 (312) 885-2480 or 882-0706

International Society of Fine Arts Appraisers Ltd., PO Box 280, River Forest, IL 60305

Mid-Am Antique Appraisers Association, PO Box 981 C.S.S., Springfield, MO 65803

New England Appraisers Association, 104 Charles Street, Boston, MA 02114 (617) 523-6272

Registered Appraisers of Florida, Inc., Box 15797, Sarasota, FL 33579, which only appraisers who work in Florida may join.

National Organizations of Antiques Dealers

National Antique and Arts Dealer Association of America
59 East 57th Street
New York, NY 10022

Antiques Dealers' Association of America
Lincoln Sanders, Membership Chairman
269 Sunset Key
Secaucus, NJ 07094

National Association of Dealers in Antiques
5859 North Main Road
Rockford, IL 01103

About the Authors

Helaine Fendelman and Jeri Schwartz joined forces in 1981 to form an arts, antiques, and household appraisal and sales firm. They have offices in Scarsdale, New York, and Stamford, Connecticut. They also write a feature column, "What Is It? What's It Worth?" for *Country Living.*

Beverly Jacobson is a free-lance writer. Her articles have appeared in *Ladies' Home Journal, Parade, Good Housekeeping,* and *The New York Times.* She is the author of YOUNG PROGRAMS FOR OLDER WORKERS.